STONE DAWN

RECLAIMING POWER FROM NARCISSIST AND TOXIC MANIPULATOR

A Guide To Self Recovery

Contents

Preface

If you're reading this, you've likely experienced the pain and confusion of narcissistic abuse. You may feel lost, broken, and unsure of your own identity. But please know that you are not alone, and there is hope for healing and recovery.

This book is a beacon of light for those who have been trapped in the darkness of narcissistic relationships. It's a roadmap to help you navigate the complexities of emotional abuse, understand the patterns of toxic behavior, and ultimately reclaim your power.

Within these pages, you will find:

- A deep dive into the psychology of narcissism and manipulation.
- Practical strategies to break free from the cycle of abuse.
- Tools to rebuild your self-esteem and confidence.
- Guidance on setting healthy boundaries and fostering positive relationships.
- Inspiration to embrace your authentic self and live a fulfilling life.

Remember, recovery is a journey, not a destination. Be patient with yourself, and celebrate every step forward. You deserve to live a life filled with love, joy, and peace.

Let's embark on this journey of healing together.

Introduction

Reclaiming Your Power: A Journey of Self-Recovery

Are the actions of a narcissist or toxic manipulator leaving you exhausted and perplexed? Have you ever questioned your sanity and worth? If so, you are not alone. Countless people throughout the world have suffered the terrible effects of narcissistic abuse, a type of psychological manipulation that may leave lasting emotional scars.

This book is your compass, guiding you through the complicated maze of narcissistic relationships and empowering you to take back your life. In these pages, you will learn about the complex dynamics of selfish behavior, the subtle strategies used to dominate and manipulate, and the tremendous influence these experiences can have on your mental and emotional well-being.

Practical guidance, insightful analysis, and real-life tales will teach you how to detect red flags, break away from the cycle of abuse, and embark on a journey of self-discovery and healing. You will learn the tools and tactics to rebuild your self-esteem, set appropriate boundaries, and cultivate strong, supportive relationships.

By the end of this book, you will be stronger, more resilient, and better prepared to live a fulfilling life free of narcissistic poison. It is time to regain control, rewrite your story, and embrace a future full of hope, happiness, and genuine connection.

1

Understanding the Dynamics

Defining Narcissism and Toxic Manipulation

Narcissism and toxic manipulation are two sinister elements that may wreak havoc on people and relationships. Narcissism, defined by an inflated sense of self-importance, a lack of empathy, and a desire for praise, frequently emerges as toxic manipulation. Toxic manipulation is an intentional method for controlling, exploiting, and undermining others.

Narcissists frequently engage in grandiose acts, believing they are superior to others. They may need continual affirmation and attention, and they may criticize or dismiss others who fail to satisfy their expectations. They may also utilize gaslighting, a manipulative technique in which they deny or distort reality to mislead and control their victims.

Toxic manipulators, whether narcissistic or not, use a wide range of strategies to obtain power and influence over others. These tactics could include:

Gaslighting is the practice of ignoring or distorting reality to cause the victim to question their sanity. For example, a poisonous manipulator may deny

2

saying anything upsetting or accuse the victim of being overly sensitive.

Guilt-tripping is the process of making the victim feel terrible about their conduct or for failing to match the manipulator's expectations. For example, a toxic manipulator would say, "You are so selfish for wanting to spend time with your friends instead of me."

Love bombing entails showering the target with attention and affection in an attempt to acquire their confidence and allegiance. Once the victim is hooked, the manipulator may withdraw affection and attention, leaving her bewildered and insecure.

Silent treatment is a form of punishment that involves ignoring or withholding communication from the victim. It can be used to control them and make them feel nervous and alone.

Projection entails projecting one's undesirable characteristics or behaviors onto others. For example, a toxic manipulator who is jealous can accuse their partner of being jealous.

It is critical to understand that narcissistic and toxic manipulative actions can be subtle and insidious. They may not always be visible, especially in the beginning phases of a relationship. However, as the relationship grows, poisonous patterns may become more noticeable.

It is also worth noting that not all narcissists are toxic manipulators, nor are all toxic manipulators narcissists. However, the two frequently go hand in hand. To maintain their inflated sense of self and exert control over others, narcissists may utilize poisonous manipulation.

Understanding the mechanics of narcissism and toxic manipulation is critical for identifying and dealing with these detrimental behaviors. Individuals who are aware of the strategies used by narcissists and toxic manipulators can defend themselves against emotional and psychological damage.

The Psychological Effects Of Narcissistic Abuse

Narcissistic abuse can have a significant and long-term influence on the victim's mental health. Constant manipulation, gaslighting, and emotional anguish can cause a variety of psychiatric disorders, including:

Victims of narcissistic abuse frequently develop persistent anxiety and despair: The persistent worry of the abuser's unexpected conduct, the sense of being watched and judged, and the loss of self-esteem can all contribute to overwhelming feelings of grief, hopelessness, and fear.

The trauma of narcissistic abuse can cause PTSD symptoms such as flashbacks, nightmares, hypervigilance, and avoidance behavior. Victims may replay the incident in their imaginations, causing severe emotional distress.

Low Self-Esteem: Narcissistic abusers frequently employ strategies to destroy their victims' self-esteem. Constant criticism, belittlement, and gaslighting can destroy the victim's sense of self, causing feelings of worthlessness and inadequacy.

Cognitive Dissonance: Narcissistic abuse can cause cognitive dissonance, a mental discomfort that happens when a person believes two or more contradicting views, ideas, or ideals. Victims may find it difficult to reconcile the abuser's warm and caring demeanor with their abusive behavior. This can cause uncertainty, skepticism, and a confused perception of reality.

Interpersonal Difficulties: Victims of narcissistic abuse may struggle to build and maintain healthy relationships due to the emotional and psychological harm caused. They may be terrified of intimacy, have trouble trusting others, and engage in codependent behaviors.

Understanding the psychological effects of narcissistic abuse is critical to healing and rehabilitation. Victims can begin to reconstruct their lives and reclaim their sense of self by recognizing trauma symptoms and obtaining professional care.

Recognizing the red flags

Identifying the signs of a toxic relationship.

Recognizing the warning signs of a toxic relationship is critical for maintaining your mental and emotional health. While it may be difficult to recognize these indications, particularly in the early phases of a relationship, paying attention to specific behaviors can help you avoid being a victim of narcissistic abuse.

Early Signs: Excessive flattery and love-bombing: Narcissists frequently lavish their victims with compliments, gifts, and attention to swiftly acquire their trust. This intensive love bombing can be overwhelming, making it difficult for the victim to recognize the red flags.

Narcissists can become jealous and possessive of their relationships, tracking their movements, controlling their social connections, and demanding constant attention.

Controlling Behavior: Narcissists frequently try to dominate their partners' decisions, finances, and social lives. They may utilize guilt-tripping, deception, or threats to achieve their objectives.

Later signs of narcissism include gaslighting and denial, where the abuser may blame the victim for their conduct. They may twist the truth, distort reality, and cause the victim to question their sanity.

Narcissists employ emotional manipulation to maintain control over their partners. They may use their emotions, such as fear, guilt, or shame, to achieve their goals.

Blaming and scapegoating: Narcissists frequently blame others for their difficulties and failures. They may blame their relationships for their misery.

Please note that not all toxic relationships have these indicators. However, if you spot multiple of these red signs, it may be time to reconsider your relationship and get help.

A Cycle of Abuse, Understanding the Pattern

Narcissistic abuse frequently follows a cyclical pattern, with phases of idealization, devaluation, rejection, and, occasionally, hoovering. Understanding this cycle might help victims identify the pattern and break free from the harmful relationship.

Idealization Phase: Love. Bombing: The narcissist lavishes the victim with care, attention, and flattery, resulting in a strong emotional relationship.

Mirroring: The narcissist reflects the victim's interests, values, and personality features, making the victim feel understood and unique.

During the devaluation phase, the narcissist criticizes and belittles the victim, causing them to lose self-esteem.

Gaslighting occurs when the narcissist manipulates the victim into doubting their senses and truth.

Silent Treatment: The narcissist may withdraw affection and attention as punishment.

Triangulation: A narcissist may use a third person to instill jealousy and insecurity.

During the Discard Phase, the narcissist may abandon the connection abruptly, leaving the victim bewildered and distraught.

During the hoovering phase (optional), the narcissist may re-engage with the victim, promising transformation and love. This hoovering phase can be especially hazardous because it can draw the victim back into the cycle of abuse.

Recognizing this recurring tendency might help victims escape the poisonous relationship. Victims can protect themselves from future emotional and psychological harm by learning the narcissist's strategies.

2

Chapter 2

Understanding Empathy and Codependency

Empathy, or the ability to comprehend and share the feelings of another, is a fundamental human trait. It enables us to connect with others on a deeper level and form lasting, meaningful relationships. However, if empathy goes unchecked, it can develop into codependency, a pattern of behavior in which one person becomes unduly dependent on another. This dynamic can be especially detrimental in interactions with narcissists because empathy can be used to manipulate and control.

Codependency is frequently found in childhood experiences, such as growing up in a dysfunctional family or being emotionally neglected. As children, we learn to adapt to our surroundings and devise coping techniques to live. Some people may become overly responsible, neglecting their own needs to suit others. These habits of behavior can persist throughout adulthood, making it difficult to build healthy, independent relationships.

Codependency in relationships with narcissists can take many forms. For instance, codependent people may:

1. Enable narcissistic behavior by making explanations or covering up the narcissist's mistakes.
2. Seek validation from the narcissist. Constantly seeking validation and confirmation.
3. Ignore their wants: They prioritize the narcissist's needs over their own.
4. Fear of abandonment: becoming unduly dependent on the narcissist for emotional support.

The dynamic between empaths and narcissists is complex. Empaths are frequently drawn to narcissists due to their allure and charisma. However, narcissists are adept manipulators who can advantage of their partners' empathy. Over time, codependent people may become locked in a cycle of abuse, feeling helpless and hopeless.

To break free from this pattern, it is critical to understand the root reasons for codependency. Individuals who recognize the patterns of conduct that contribute to codependency might begin to heal and recover. This process may include seeking treatment, practicing self-care, and setting healthy limits.

The Cycle of Codependency

Codependency, a complicated pattern of behavior, is frequently caused by deep-rooted emotional demands and fears. It is a disorder marked by an obsessive need to control others, please others, and seek validation from outside sources. This habit can emerge in a variety of ways, often resulting in toxic or dysfunctional relationships.

Enabling Behavior: Enabling conduct is a key aspect of codependency. This happens when someone encourages or excuses another person's poor or destructive behavior. Codependents in narcissistic relationships may justify the narcissist's acts, accept responsibility for their faults, or give them resources that allow them to engage in damaging behavior. This can vary from cash assistance to emotional validation. By enabling the narcissist, the codependent continues the abuse cycle and prevents the narcissist from accepting responsibility for their actions.

Fear of abandonment: Deep-seated anxieties of abandonment might exacerbate codependency. Even a harmful or destructive relationship may be necessary for people who have been hurt or rejected. Fear can lead to a frantic clinging to the narcissist, who may believe they are the only person capable of providing love and support. People-pleasing is also a prevalent characteristic of codependency. Codependents frequently put the wants and desires of others before their own. They may make tremendous efforts to avoid disagreement or rejection, even if it means giving up their happiness. This conduct might cause feelings of resentment, irritation, and burnout.

Low self-esteem is a common contributing factor to codependency. Individuals with poor self-esteem may question their worth and believe that they are unworthy of affection and respect. As a result, they may seek approval from others, especially narcissistic spouses. This might trigger a cycle of self-doubt and self-sabotage.

Setting Boundaries Reclaiming Your Power.

Setting boundaries is a critical step toward overcoming codependency and reclaiming your authority. Boundaries are restrictions that you establish to preserve your physical, emotional, and mental health. They help you form healthy connections and retain your sense of self.

Identifying personal boundaries: The first step in setting limits is to determine your values and beliefs. What are the things you will not compromise on? What are you willing to accept, and what are you not? Once you have a firm grasp of your values, you can start setting boundaries that are consistent with them.

Communicating boundaries: assertively Establishing your boundaries assertively is critical. This is communicating your demands and desires clearly and frankly, without being confrontational or passive-aggressive. Use "I" phrases to describe your feelings rather than blaming or accusing others. Instead of stating, "You always do this to me," you could add, "I feel hurt when you do this."

Enforcing limits: Setting limits can be difficult, especially if you are accustomed to pleasing others. However, it is critical to maintain your boundaries, even if it means disappointing others. Be prepared to say no and to place limitations on your time and energy.

Dealing with boundary violations: When someone crosses your limits, you should respond calmly and assertively. Say you won't tolerate their behavior. If required, you may need to separate yourself from the individual or terminate the relationship.

Setting and enforcing boundaries allows you to recover your authority and foster healthier relationships. You have the right to decline, set limits, and prioritize your needs.

Cultivating Self-Compassion: Healing Past Wounds.

Self-compassion is the discipline of treating oneself with kindness, understanding, and acceptance. It entails admitting your flaws, acknowledging your pain, and offering yourself support and encouragement. Self-compassion can help you heal old wounds and develop a better sense of self.

Practicing self-kindness: Self-compassion is a basic component of self-compassion. This entails treating oneself with the same care and understanding that you would extend to a friend. When you make a mistake or face a setback, be kind to yourself. Instead of criticizing yourself, be encouraging and supportive.

Let Go of Self-Criticism: Self-criticism is a typical tendency that can harm your confidence and well-being. Recognize and fight negative self-talk. Replace self-critical ideas with compassionate ones. For example, instead of thinking, "I am such a failure," consider, "Everyone makes errors. I can benefit from this experience."

Embracing imperfection: Nobody is perfect, so it is necessary to embrace your flaws. By accepting your shortcomings, you can relieve yourself of the burden of being flawless. Remember that it is okay to make mistakes. In reality, mistakes can provide excellent learning opportunities.

Forgiving yourself: Forgiveness is a vital step in the healing process. If you have made mistakes in the past, you should forgive yourself. Holding onto guilt and shame will only impede your progress and happiness. Practice self-forgiveness by admitting your mistakes, learning from them, and moving on.

Breaking free from the victim mentality.

A victim mentality can stifle personal development and prevent you from taking charge of your life. It is a way of thinking that focuses on external factors and blames others for your issues. To break away from this thinking, change your perspective and accept responsibility for your happiness.

Taking responsibility: The first step toward breaking away from the victim attitude is accepting responsibility for your actions and decisions. Instead of blaming others, accept responsibility for your circumstances. You shouldn't ignore others' harm but rather focus on what you can control.

Shifting your perspective: Reframing adverse situations can help you change your perspective. Instead of focusing on the negative parts of a situation, look for the silver lining. Look for opportunities for growth and learning, even in the most difficult situations.

Empowering Yourself: To overcome the victim attitude, you must first empower yourself. This includes taking action, establishing objectives, and following your aspirations. Believe in your ability, and do not let fear stop you.

Building Self-Confidence: Self-confidence is vital for overcoming the victim's attitude. Focus on your qualities and successes to boost your self-confidence. Celebrate your accomplishments, no matter how minor they may appear. Surround yourself with positive individuals who believe in you.

3

Chapter 3

Understanding Emotional Attachment

Emotional connection is a complicated psychological bond that exists between people. It is a natural human desire to seek connection and closeness, but when these attachments become excessive or toxic, they can stifle personal progress and well-being. Understanding the nature of emotional attachment is critical for getting out of toxic relationships and creating healthier ones.

Emotional attachment is driven by a fear of loss. When we grow deeply connected to someone or something, we are afraid of losing them or being rejected. This dread can take many forms, including clinginess, jealousy, and dominating behavior. It can also lead to feelings of desperation and a willingness to sacrifice one's wants and principles to keep the connection.

Neediness and dependency are intimately related to emotional attachment. When we feel uncomfortable or inadequate, we may go to others to confirm our worth and satisfy our emotional needs. This can result in a codependent dynamic in which both couples become unduly reliant on one another. As a result, people may sacrifice their ambitions and goals to satisfy their partners, resulting in resentment and discontent.

To stop the pattern of emotional attachment, it is critical to identify and address the underlying fears and insecurities that drive these actions. We can nurture a sense of self-worth and autonomy by first understanding our wants and desires better. This enables us to establish healthy relationships built on mutual respect, trust, and independence.

Practice Emotional Detachment

To create emotional detachment, it is necessary to practice mindfulness, which is being present in the moment. By focusing on the present moment rather than obsessing over the past or worrying about the future, we can lessen emotional reactivity and make more deliberate decisions.

Cognitive restructuring is another effective technique for developing emotional detachment. This entails detecting and correcting harmful thought patterns that promote emotional attachment. By replacing these beliefs with more realistic and pleasant ones, we may change our emotional state and break free from unhealthy behaviors.

Setting limits is critical for maintaining our emotional well-being. It entails creating clear boundaries for what we are willing to tolerate in our relationships. We can avoid feelings of overload and resentment by assertively communicating our needs and expectations. It is critical to remember that setting limits is not selfish; it is a kind of self-care.

Limiting interaction with toxic people can greatly lessen emotional triggers. We can promote healing and growth by reducing our exposure to negative stimuli. Depending on the severity of the situation, this could entail decreasing communication, establishing tougher limits, or perhaps terminating relations completely.

This process requires patience and compassion. Emotional detachment is a talent that requires time and practice to achieve. By persistently implementing these tactics, we can progressively break free from the bonds of emotional attachment and establish healthier, more meaningful relationships.

Building Emotional Resilience

Developing emotional resilience is critical for overcoming life's obstacles and maintaining emotional well-being. Self-compassion is a key component of resilience. By treating ourselves with kindness and empathy, we can lessen self-criticism and increase our sense of self-worth. When we are sympathetic to ourselves, we are better prepared to deal with setbacks and disappointments.

Building self-esteem is another important aspect of emotional resilience. Recognizing our skills and accomplishments might help us develop a positive self-image. This includes setting reasonable objectives, enjoying our accomplishments, and learning from our mistakes. When we believe in ourselves, we are more likely to overcome adversity.

Effective stress management practices are required to preserve emotional balance. Meditation, yoga, and deep breathing are all effective methods for reducing stress and anxiety. Physical activity, enough sleep, and a nutritious diet are all beneficial for stress management. Prioritizing self-care can increase our general well-being and ability to deal with obstacles.

A solid support system is essential for developing resilience. Surrounding ourselves with pleasant and helpful people can provide us with motivation, empathy, and practical help. Sharing our feelings with trusted friends and family members can help reduce stress and promote emotional healing. Joining support groups or seeking professional counseling can also offer essential assistance and insight.

We can develop the resilience required to endure life's problems and thrive by fostering self-compassion, increasing self-esteem, adopting stress management strategies, and cultivating positive relationships.

The Power of No: Assert Yourself and Set Limits

A key skill for emotional detachment is saying "no." We often feel bound to please others, even if it means sacrificing our own needs and well-being. However, by learning to express ourselves and create boundaries, we may protect our emotional energy while maintaining healthy relationships.

Communicating assertively entails expressing one's opinions and feelings openly and politely. This entails using "I" phrases to communicate our needs and objectives without blaming or accusing others. It is critical to be direct and honest while simultaneously being sensitive to the other person's sentiments.

Overcoming the fear of disagreement is critical to establishing ourselves. While conflict might be unpleasant, it is a normal element of human contact. By addressing conflict with a calm and rational perspective, we can resolve it peacefully and sustain healthy relationships. Listen to the other person's point of view and seek common ground.

Saying "no" without guilt can be difficult, but it is an important ability. When we feel compelled to answer "yes" to every request, we risk becoming overwhelmed and resentful. Learning to decline respectfully and confidently allows us to avoid unneeded stress and maintain our well-being. It is crucial to remember that it is acceptable to prioritize our own needs.

Setting boundaries with problematic individuals can be especially difficult. However, it is critical for maintaining our emotional wellness. We can mitigate the harmful effects of toxic relationships by setting clear boundaries for what we are ready to endure. It is critical to be firm and consistent in setting boundaries, even if it means abandoning the relationship.

We may empower ourselves and create healthier relationships by mastering the art of saying "no," talking assertively, overcoming conflict avoidance, and setting boundaries.

Moving Forward and Embracing a New Chapter

Letting go of the past is critical for moving forward. This entails releasing bitterness, wrath, and other negative emotions that may be keeping us back. We can break free from the burdens of the past by forgiving ourselves and others.

Accepting change can be difficult, but it is an essential element of progress. By embracing new experiences and possibilities, we might broaden our horizons and discover new interests. It is critical to be open to change and adapt to new situations.

Cultivating hope and optimism is essential for a positive attitude. By focusing on the positive aspects of our lives, we can change our perspective and attract more positive events. It is critical to cultivate thankfulness and find delight in the little things.

Celebrating our progress is critical for staying motivated. Recognizing our accomplishments, no matter how modest can help us enhance our self-esteem and continue on track. It is critical to reward ourselves for our efforts and celebrate our achievements.

We can begin a new chapter in our lives full of joy, fulfillment, and peace by letting go of the past, embracing change, nurturing hope and optimism, and celebrating our progress.

4

Chapter 4

Rediscovering Your Self-Worth

Self-worth is the cornerstone of our lives. It is a belief in our own worth, competency, and capacity to navigate the world. When self-esteem is high, we are more robust, confident, and capable of dealing with life's difficulties. In contrast, poor self-worth can lead to feelings of inadequacy, insecurity, and self-doubt.

Narcissistic abuse can significantly lower our self-esteem. Constant criticism, gaslighting, and manipulation can undermine our sense of self and cause us to question reality. It is critical to understand the consequences of this abuse and take action to recover our self-esteem.

One of the first tasks is to recognize and confront negative self-talk. Narcissistic abusers frequently employ negative rhetoric to discredit their victims. They may insult you, dismiss your successes, or make you feel useless. Over time, these negative messages might get internalized, resulting in a negative self-image.

To overcome negative self-talk, we must become more conscious of our thoughts and question their reality. Are these ideas based on fact or fiction? Are they beneficial or harmful? Once we have identified negative thoughts, we can replace them with beneficial ones. For example, rather than thinking, "I am not good enough," we can reply, "I am capable and worthy of love and respect."

Celebrating our accomplishments, no matter how modest, is another vital step toward rebuilding our self-esteem. Too frequently, we focus on our shortcomings while ignoring our accomplishments. It is critical to recognize our accomplishments, large and small, and to credit ourselves for our hard work and dedication.

When we celebrate our accomplishments, we boost our confidence in our own skills. We start to regard ourselves as capable and competent people. This positive self-perception can help us overcome obstacles and achieve our objectives.

It is also crucial to learn how to politely take praise. When someone compliments us, we may feel compelled to minimize our accomplishments or ignore their praise. However, praises should be accepted with appreciation and humility.

Accepting compliments acknowledges our worth and value. We are also showing others that we value their pleasant words. Accepting praise gracefully can increase our self-esteem and foster closer relationships with others.

In addition to enjoying our accomplishments and accepting accolades, we must combat imposter syndrome. Imposter syndrome is the idea that we are not as capable or intelligent as others think we are. We may feel like frauds or impostors, constantly on the verge of being discovered.

Imposter syndrome is particularly common among exceptional performers. We may have high expectations for ourselves and feel that we are never satisfactory enough. It is vital to realize that everyone has self-doubt. Even the most successful individuals experience periods of insecurity.

To overcome the imposter syndrome, we must confront our self-doubt and negative thoughts. Are these views founded on truth or fiction? Are they beneficial or harmful? Once we have identified negative beliefs, we can replace them with beneficial ones.

It is also vital to accept vulnerability and imperfection. Nobody is flawless, and it is acceptable to make mistakes. In fact, making mistakes can provide excellent learning opportunities. By accepting our flaws, we can become more robust and confident.

When we believe in ourselves, we are more likely to take chances, pursue our objectives, and lead satisfying lives. By regaining our own worth, we may break out from the cycle of narcissistic abuse and build a better future for ourselves.

Prioritizing self-care.

Self-care is sometimes ignored, especially when we are preoccupied with taking care of others. However, it is critical to our total well-being. When we disregard our own needs, we become drained and unable to provide adequate care for others.

Physical Self-Care.

Physical self-care entails taking care of our body. This involves getting enough sleep, eating a nutritious diet, and exercising frequently. When we prioritize physical self-care, we gain energy, improve our mood, and fortify our immune systems.

Getting enough sleep is critical to our physical and mental well-being. When we sleep well, we are more awake, focused, and productive. Aim to get 7-8 hours of sleep each night.

Eating nutritious food is another critical component of physical self-care. Consuming a variety of fruits, vegetables, and whole grains can help us maintain a healthy weight, lower our risk of chronic diseases, and increase our energy levels.

Regular exercise is also beneficial to our physical health. Exercise improves our cardiovascular health, strengthens our muscles and bones, and relieves stress. Aim for at least 30 minutes of moderate-intensity exercise on most days of the week.

In addition to these essential requirements, it is critical to incorporate relaxing techniques into our everyday routines. Yoga, meditation, and deep breathing are all effective ways to relieve stress, boost mood, and encourage better sleep.

Emotional Self-Care.

Emotional self-care entails taking care of our emotional needs. This includes properly processing our feelings, receiving help from loved ones, and practicing self-compassion.

It is critical to recognize and process our emotions, both positive and negative. Suppressing our emotions might result in mental distress and physical health issues. Find appropriate ways to vent your emotions, such as journaling, speaking with a friend, or seeking professional help.

Building positive ties with loved ones is also beneficial to emotional well-being. Spending time with individuals who care about us might make us feel more supported and valued.

Self-compassion is another essential component of emotional self-care. Be gentle with yourself, particularly when you make errors. Remember that everyone makes mistakes, and it is acceptable to be imperfect.

Mental Self-Care.

Mental self-care entails taking care of one's mental health. This includes engaging in mentally stimulating activities, challenging oneself, and limiting exposure to negative influences.

Hobbies and creative activities can help us relax, reduce stress, and improve our mood. Finding hobbies you enjoy, such as painting, writing, playing a musical instrument, or gardening, might help you maintain your mental health.

Learning new abilities and challenging oneself can help us maintain our mental sharpness. Taking a class, learning a new language, or volunteering can all contribute to our personal growth and development.

It is critical to restrict our exposure to negative influences, such as adverse news and social media. These can all lead to emotions of tension, worry, and sadness.

Prioritizing self-care allows us to improve our overall well-being and live a more rewarding lifestyle. Remember that taking care of oneself is not selfish; it is vital.

Practicing mindfulness.

Mindfulness is the practice of remaining present in the moment. It entails paying attention to our ideas, feelings, and sensations without passing judgment. Mindfulness can help us reduce stress, improve focus, and enhance our overall well-being.

Understanding Mindfulness

Mindfulness is commonly connected with meditation, although it may be applied to any aspect of our lives. Simply paying attention to our breath, senses, and surroundings can help us become more attentive.

When we are conscious, we are completely present in the moment. We do not dwell on the past or worry about the future. Instead, we concentrate on the here and now.

Mindfulness techniques

There are numerous mindfulness practices that you can try. Here are some popular ones:

Meditation: Meditation entails sitting silently and concentrating on your breath. You can also concentrate on a mantra or a particular object.

Mindful breathing: means paying attention to your breath as it enters and exits your body. Feel the rise and fall of your chest.

Mindful walking: entails paying attention to the sensation of your feet touching the ground. Take in the sights, sounds, and fragrances around you.

Mindful eating: involves paying attention to the taste, smell, and texture of your food. Eat gently and relish every bite.

Integrating mindfulness into daily life.

Mindfulness can be applied to any part of your life. Here are some tips:

Mindful eating involves paying attention to the taste, smell, and texture of your food. Eat gently and relish every bite.

Mindful walking entails paying attention to the sensation of your feet touching the ground. Take in the sights, sounds, and fragrances around you.

Mindful communication means paying attention to your words and how they may affect others. Listen intently and reply thoughtfully.

Mindful parenting is being present with your children. Play with them, listen to them, and demonstrate that you care.

Mindfulness can help us reduce stress, improve focus, and improve our overall well-being. It is a simple but effective technique that can help us live more satisfying lives.

Heal Your Inner Child.

Our inner child is the portion of ourselves that carries the wounds and traumas from our childhood. These scars can manifest in a variety of ways, including low self-esteem, fear of abandonment, and difficulties developing meaningful relationships.

Identifying your inner child

To repair your inner child, first identify the scars and traumas you are carrying. This can be an unpleasant procedure, but it is necessary for recovery.

Here are some questions you can ask yourself:

1. What were your main caretakers like?
2. Were they emotionally available and supportive?

3. Have you been through any serious trauma, such as abuse, neglect, or loss?
4. What are your fundamental ideas about yourself?
5. Are they favorable or negative?

After you have discovered your inner child's wounds, you may start the healing process.

Nurture Your Inner Child

Nurturing your inner child entails treating oneself with the same love, compassion, and understanding that you would show a kid. Here are a few tips:

1. Practice self-compassion. Be gentle with yourself, particularly when you make errors.
2. Forgive yourself. Let go of previous mistakes and forgive yourself for any transgression.
3. Engage in child-like activities: Do activities that make you happy, such as playing games, watching cartoons, or coloring.
4. Spend time in nature. Nature provides a relaxing and therapeutic impact.
5. Seek expert help. If you are having trouble healing your inner child on your own, you should consider seeing a therapist.
6. Nurturing your inner child allows you to heal old traumas and live a more satisfying life.
7. Embracing your authentic self entails being true to yourself, no matter what others may think. It is about respecting your uniqueness and leading a life that is consistent with your values and interests.
8. Discovering Your True Self To embrace your real self, you must first identify who you truly are. This entails discovering your values, passions,

and strengths.

Here are some questions you can ask yourself:

1. What are my core values?
2. What am I enthusiastic about?
3. What are my strengths and weaknesses?
4. What are my dreams and goals?

Once you have a greater understanding of yourself, you can start living more authentically.

Expressing Your Authentic Self

Speaking your truth, creating boundaries, and living a life that reflects your values are all part of expressing your authentic self.

Here are some tips to convey your real self:

1. **Speak the truth:** Do not be scared to express your thoughts, even if it means going against the grain.
2. **Set boundaries:** Learn to say no to things that do not benefit you.
3. **Live a life with purpose.** Find something you are enthusiastic about and pursue it wholeheartedly.
4. **Surround yourself with positive individuals:** Spend time with people who will support and encourage you.

Overcoming Fear of Judgment.

Fear of being judged is one of the most difficult aspects of embracing your genuine self. However, remember that you are not responsible for others' opinions.

Here are some ideas for overcoming your fear of judgment:

1. **Develop self-confidence:** Believe in your ability.
2. **Practice self-acceptance:** Accept yourself as you are, warts and all.
3. **Let go of the urge for approval:** Stop seeking validation from others.
4. **Focus on your happiness:** Do whatever makes you happy, not what others expect you to do.
5. **Living a more full and meaningful life:** requires you to embrace your genuine self.

5

Chapter 5

Setting Healthy Boundaries

Understanding Boundaries

The concept of boundaries, which is sometimes disregarded or misinterpreted, is critical to developing and maintaining good relationships. A boundary is a limit or expectation we have for ourselves and others. It is a method of ensuring our emotional, physical, and mental well-being. Clear limits allow us to successfully convey our needs and expectations, lowering the possibility of misunderstandings and disputes.

In the case of narcissistic and toxic relationships, boundaries are especially important. These people frequently thrive on pushing boundaries and exploiting vulnerabilities. Setting and enforcing boundaries allows us to defend ourselves from their manipulative tactics and regain control of our lives.

To set appropriate limits, we must first understand our own needs and values. What are our limitations? What actions are we willing to tolerate? Reflecting on these issues can help us understand what we need to defend.

Communicating boundaries clearly and assertively

When we have a firm awareness of our limits, the next step is to effectively convey them. This necessitates aggressive communication, which entails expressing our wants and desires clearly and politely. It is critical to avoid passive-aggressive behavior and people-pleasing, as these approaches will only lead to resentment and dissatisfaction.

Instead of expressing, "I am feeling overwhelmed," we could add, "I need some time alone right now." "I will be available later." This straightforward statement eliminates the possibility of misinterpretation and establishes a healthy barrier.

It is equally critical to employ "I" phrases to express our emotions and desires. This helps you avoid blaming or accusing people. For example, instead of stating, "You always make me feel bad," we could say, "I am hurt when you say things like that."

Enforcing boundaries.

Setting boundaries is just the first step. The true test is to enforce them. This demands boldness and consistency. When someone exceeds a boundary, it is critical to respond gently and decisively. We can utilize aggressive communication to communicate our displeasure and reinforce our expectations.

If someone continues to ignore our boundaries, we may need to take more serious measures, such as limiting contact or quitting the relationship entirely. This can be a challenging decision, but it is necessary for our well-being.

Remember that maintaining limits does not imply being selfish or unkind. It is about self-respect and survival. Setting and enforcing limits can lead to happier and more fulfilling relationships.

Communicating effectively

Active Listening.

Effective communication is an essential component of healthy partnerships. It entails not just sharing our own ideas and emotions but also actively listening to others. Active listening necessitates our complete focus, empathy, and understanding.

When we attentively listen, we are not only hearing the words uttered but also observing the speaker's tone of voice, body language, and underlying emotions. Tuning into these nonverbal clues allows us to obtain a better comprehension of the message being presented.

To practice active listening, we can:

Maintain eye contact: This demonstrates that we are engaged and interested.

Avoid interruptions: Allow the speaker to complete their thoughts before answering.

To ensure understanding, we should paraphrase the speaker's message.

Ask clarifying questions. Seek additional information to clear up any confusion.

Validate the speaker's feelings. Recognize and empathize with their emotions.

By attentively listening, we can increase trust, settle disagreements, and deepen our relationships.

Assertive Communication

Assertive communication entails expressing our opinions and feelings truthfully and clearly while also respecting the rights and sentiments of others. It is a balance between passive and aggressive behavior.

Passive communication entails avoiding disagreement and putting the needs of others ahead of our own. This might cause resentment and disappointment. Aggressive communication, on the other hand, is about dominating and controlling others. This can harm relationships and foster resentment.

In contrast, assertive communication helps us to express ourselves truthfully while also advocating for our demands. It includes:

Using "I" statements: This allows us to take control of our emotions and avoid blaming others.

Expressing our needs and desires clearly: This decreases the possibility of misunderstanding.

Setting limits protects both our emotional and physical well-being.

Responding quietly and respectfully helps de-escalate a confrontation.

Assertive communication can help us enhance our relationships and minimize stress.

Non-verbal communication

Body language, often known as nonverbal communication, is an important aspect of how we interact with others. Our facial expressions, gestures, and posture can convey information that words cannot.

Some important features of nonverbal communication include:

Facial Expressions: Our facial expressions can disclose our emotions, including happiness, sadness, rage, and surprise.

Eye Contact: Maintaining eye contact demonstrates interest and attentiveness.

Posture might indicate confidence or insecurity.

Gestures can highlight words or express unique meanings.

Tone of speech: Our tone of voice can express our emotions and attitudes.

By paying attention to our own and others' nonverbal clues, we can enhance our communication skills and strengthen our relationships.

Conflict Resolution

Conflict is a normal aspect of any relationship, but how we handle it has a huge impact on the result. Effective conflict resolution requires open communication, empathy, and a willingness to compromise.

Active listening is one of the most crucial abilities for conflict resolution. By sincerely listening to the other person, we can obtain a better grasp of their feelings and needs. This can assist in de-escalating the situation and open up a more fruitful discourse.

Another key ability is forceful communication. When we express our feelings and needs assertively, we avoid passive-aggressive conduct and reduce misunderstandings. It is critical to utilize "I" phrases to focus on our own emotions and avoid blaming the other person.

When a conflict emerges, it is critical to resolve it quickly. Avoiding the problem or hoping it goes away will only make it worse. Instead, set aside a time to chat when both sides are calm and can concentrate on the problem at hand.

During the conversation, it is critical to stay focused on the topic and avoid personal attacks. Try to see the situation from the other person's eyes and find common ground. Be open to compromise and find a solution that benefits both parties.

If the conflict is extremely intense, it may be beneficial to consult with a mediator or therapist. These professionals can create a neutral environment in which both parties can vent their emotions and work toward a solution.

Remember that disagreement is not always terrible. It may provide an opportunity for growth and better understanding. By approaching confrontation with a positive attitude and a willingness to compromise, we can deepen our relationships and come out stronger.

Choose Recognizing Red Flags: A Smart Approach

When starting a new relationship, it is critical to be aware of the warning signs that may indicate a toxic or abusive dynamic. These red flags might appear in a variety of ways, including:

1. **Controlling Behavior:** This can involve attempts to restrict your social connections, track your movements, or make decisions for you.
2. **Excessive jealousy and possessiveness** can indicate feelings of insecurity and control.
3. **Gaslighting** is a type of manipulation in which the abuser attempts to undermine your views and reality.
4. **Hot and cold behavior** refers to alternating periods of strong attachment

and neglect or disengagement.

5. **Blaming and shaming:** The abuser may accuse you of their own mistakes or criticize you to make you feel inferior.

If you see these warning signs in a possible mate, trust your intuition and take precautions to protect yourself.

Self-Reflection

Before starting a new relationship, it is vital to reflect on yourself. Think about your wants, values, and boundaries. What attributes do you search for in a partner? What are your deal breakers?

Understanding yourself better allows you to make more educated judgments about who you spend time with. Also, be honest with yourself about your habits and tendencies. Are you drawn to toxic relationships? Do you have a people-pleasing or codependent personality?

By resolving these difficulties, you can break away from negative habits and attract healthier relationships.

Compatibility Check

Compatibility is a vital aspect of any relationship. While attractiveness and chemistry are vital, you should also consider common values, aspirations, and interests.

When determining compatibility, examine the following questions:

1. Do you have comparable values and beliefs?
2. Are your communication styles compatible?
3. Do you have comparable life objectives and aspirations?

4. Do you enjoy spending time together and discussing mutual interests?

Consider these things to boost your chances of finding a spouse who is compatible with you.

Establishing Strong Support Systems.

Cultivating positive relationships

A solid support system is critical to our emotional and mental well-being. Surrounding oneself with good, helpful individuals can help us overcome life's obstacles and enjoy our accomplishments.

To build positive relationships, we can:

1. **Become a trustworthy friend:** Support, empathize, and encourage others.
2. **Practice active listening:** Pay attention to what people say and how they feel.
3. **Be dependable:** Keep your promises and be there for others when they need you.
4. **Be honest and sincere.** Stay honest with yourself and others.
5. **Forgive and let go:** Holding grudges can harm relationships.

By developing strong, healthy relationships, we may create a network of support that will help us get through difficult times.

Joining support groups.

Joining a support group can be an effective method to connect with others who have had similar experiences. Support groups offer a secure and helpful environment in which we may express our emotions, learn from others, and be encouraged.

When selecting a support group, it is critical to locate one that matches your needs and interests. You may wish to investigate the group's emphasis, size, and meeting frequency.

Once you have found a support group, talk openly and honestly about your experiences. Express your feelings and ask inquiries. By actively engaging in the group, you can obtain vital knowledge and assistance.

Seeking mentorship.

A mentor can offer counsel, direction, and support as we traverse our personal and professional lives. A mentor can help us set objectives, overcome obstacles, and realize our full potential.

Consider reaching out to people you admire or respect. To meet possible mentors, consider joining professional organizations or volunteer groups.

When developing a mentoring relationship, it is critical to be respectful, appreciative, and open to feedback. Ask thoughtful questions, show initiative, and be open to learning.

Seeking mentorship allows us to get useful insights and accelerate our development.

Developing Healthy Relationships with Family and Friends.

Setting boundaries with the family

Family relationships may be complicated, particularly when there are unresolved issues or toxic dynamics. Setting boundaries with family members can be challenging, but it is critical for our mental and emotional well-being.

To establish healthy limits with family, communicate your wants and expectations clearly and assertively.

1. Set limitations for what we are willing to tolerate.
2. Maintain our boundaries constantly.
3. Take care of yourself and avoid pleasing others.
4. Limit your interactions with harmful family members if necessary.

Setting and enforcing boundaries allows us to protect ourselves from emotional and psychological harm.

repairing damaged relationships.

Broken relationships are unpleasant, but they may be mended with time, effort, and forgiveness. To mend a shattered relationship, we can accept responsibility for our actions.

1. I sincerely apologize.
2. Listen actively and compassionately.
3. Communicate freely and honestly.
4. Practice forgiveness.

It is vital to understand that not all relationships can be repaired. Sometimes it is vital to end poisonous relationships for our good.

Nurturing friendships

Friendships are a valuable source of support and satisfaction. To strengthen our friendships, we might prioritize them.

1. Be a skilled listener.
2. Provide support and encouragement.
3. Be dependable and trustworthy.
4. Spend some quality time together.

We can build our friendships and form long-lasting connections by devoting time and attention to them.

6

Chapter 6

Understanding the Power of Forgiveness

Forgiveness, a sometimes misunderstood and underestimated concept, is a powerful tool that has the potential to improve people's lives. It is not just an emotional act but a deliberate decision with significant psychological and spiritual rewards. While it may appear contradictory, forgiveness is not about condoning unlawful action or downplaying the grief caused. Instead, it is about letting go of resentment and wrath and freeing oneself from the emotional burdens of the past.

The science of forgiveness demonstrates its significant impact on our well-being. When we harbor resentment, our bodies maintain a state of chronic stress by releasing stress chemicals, such as cortisol. Chronic stress can cause a variety of physical and mental health issues, including heart disease, high blood pressure, anxiety, and depression. Forgiveness, on the other hand, causes the production of oxytocin, also known as the "love hormone," which fosters feelings of calm, compassion, and trust.

The advantages of forgiving go beyond physical wellness. It has the potential to greatly improve our connections with others as well as ourselves. When we forgive someone, we create an opportunity for reconciliation and understanding. It enables us to restore damaged connections and strengthen bonds. Furthermore, forgiveness might improve our self-esteem and worth. By letting go of resentment, we break free from the bonds of self-blame and guilt. This newfound freedom enables us to embrace our genuine selves and live authentically.

Forgiveness is not a one-time event but an ongoing process. It takes perseverance, effort, and a desire to let go of the past. It is vital to remember that forgiveness is not about forgetting the hurt but about refusing to let it govern our lives. By forgiving others, we can eventually forgive ourselves.

Let go of resentment and anger.

Resentment and anger, like unwelcome guests, can stay in our hearts long after the initial pain has subsided. These negative feelings can take over our thinking, distort our judgment, and poison our relationships. To fully experience the transformative power of forgiveness, we must first learn to let go of these damaging emotions.

Unmet expectations, perceived injustices, and prior traumas are common causes of resentment and wrath. When our desires or beliefs are violated, we may become angry and frustrated. Over time, these feelings can develop into resentment, a deep-seated animosity that can harm our mental and emotional health.

The circle of resentment is destructive. It starts with a perceived wrong, which leads to sentiments of rage and hurt. If left uncontrolled, these emotions might develop into resentment, resulting in unpleasant thoughts and behaviors. These negative ideas, in turn, fuel resentment and prolong the cycle.

To break free from this cycle, we must first recognize the presence of resentment and hatred in ourselves. This might be a difficult undertaking since we may be tempted to deny or repress our emotions. However, honest self-reflection is necessary for recovery.

Once we have acknowledged our feelings, we may start to let them go. Journaling is a useful technique. Writing about our sentiments allows us to develop a better grasp of our ideas and emotions. This method can help us uncover the underlying roots of our resentment and anger, as well as remove the negative energy linked with these emotions.

Meditation and mindfulness practices can also help you let go of resentment and wrath. We can relax and relieve stress by focusing on the current moment. This can help us become more compassionate and forgiving toward ourselves and others.

It is vital to realize that getting rid of bitterness and anger is not always simple. It may need time and work, but it is ultimately worthwhile. By releasing these negative feelings, we can find more peace, joy, and fulfillment in our lives.

Practice Forgiveness: A Step-by-Step Guide

Forgiveness is a journey, not a destination. It takes intentional effort and a desire to let go of the past. While the process is tough, it is also satisfying. Here's a step-by-step strategy for practicing forgiveness:

Step One: Acknowledge the Hurt

The first step toward forgiveness is acknowledging the grief created by the cruel behavior. This could include confronting tough feelings like anger, despair, or betrayal. Recognizing the hurt validates our feelings and marks the first step toward healing.

Step 2: Understand the other person's perspective.

Although it may be challenging, try to grasp the other person's point of view. This does not imply condoning or justifying their behavior. Rather, it entails attempting to comprehend the underlying motivations behind their conduct. Empathy for the other person allows us to let go of resentment and anger.

Step 3: Let go of the need for revenge.

The urge for vengeance might keep us stuck in a cycle of negativity. By letting go of the need for vengeance, we relieve ourselves of the emotional burden of wrath and bitterness. Instead of pursuing retaliation, we might concentrate on healing and progress.

Step 4: Practice self-compassion.

Forgiveness is not only about forgiving others but also about forgiving oneself. Be gentle and sympathetic with yourself, and avoid self-blame and guilt. Remember that everyone makes mistakes, so learn from them rather than dwell on them.

Step 5: Forgive yourself.

Forgiveness requires reciprocation. We must forgive ourselves just as much as we do others. Admit your mistakes, learn from them, and let go of guilt and shame.

Remember: Forgiveness does not imply ignoring the past. It is about refusing to let it dominate your present and future. By practicing forgiveness, we can find more peace, joy, and fulfillment in our lives.

Moving Forward: Embracing a Future Free of the Past

Once we have forgiven, the next step is to go forward. This entails breaking free from the past and welcoming a future full of promise and possibility.

To fully move forward, we must first break free from the patterns and behaviors that bind us to the past. This could include changing our routines, relationships, or even our surroundings. By separating ourselves from the root of our grief, we may make room for healing and progress.

Creating a new narrative is a vital step toward moving on. This entails reframing our past experiences and cultivating a positive vision for the future. Instead of dwelling on the negative, we should focus on the lessons learned and future opportunities.

Setting limits is critical to protecting ourselves from potential harm. Setting clear and healthy boundaries allows us to build healthy relationships and avoid toxic circumstances. It is critical to communicate our limits assertively and respectfully and to consistently enforce them.

By breaking free from the past, developing a new story, and establishing healthy boundaries, we may embrace a future full of promise and possibility. Remember that the past is gone, but the future is ours to shape.

Finding Peace: Accepting Imperfection.

One of the most significant barriers to forgiveness and moving on is the quest for perfection. We frequently seek immaculate relationships, perfect situations, and ideal results. However, this pursuit might result in disappointment, anger, and hatred.

To achieve true serenity, we must accept imperfection. This entails recognizing that mistakes are a normal part of life and that no one is flawless. By letting go of the drive for perfection, we can lessen tension and anxiety while improving our general well-being.

Cultivating thankfulness is another effective method for achieving serenity. By focusing on the positive aspects of our lives, we can change our perspective and lessen unpleasant feelings. Gratitude may help us appreciate even the little things, such as excellent health, loving relationships, and beautiful scenery.

We can achieve long-term calm and contentment by accepting imperfections and nurturing thankfulness. Remember, happiness is a journey, not a destination.

7

Chapter 7

The impact of positive thinking on mental health

Positive thinking, a mental attitude that focuses on the positive aspects of life, has a significant impact on our mental health. It is more than just a cliché or a feel-good phrase; it is a scientifically established method for improving our well-being. By adopting a positive mindset, we may improve our emotional condition, reduce stress, and increase general happiness.

One of the primary ways that positive thinking improves our mental health is by affecting brain chemistry. When we think of pleasant ideas, our brain releases neurotransmitters such as dopamine and serotonin, also known as "feel-good" hormones. Dopamine is related to pleasure and reward, whereas serotonin promotes emotions of happiness and well-being. Positive thinking can help ease symptoms of sadness and anxiety by raising neurotransmitter levels in the brain.

Furthermore, optimistic thinking has been linked to lower stress levels. When we face problems, negative thoughts can intensify our stress response, resulting in elevated cortisol levels. Cortisol, sometimes known as the "stress hormone," can have negative impacts on both our physical and emotional health. However, by maintaining a cheerful attitude, we can lessen the effects of stress. Positive thinking allows us to reinterpret difficult situations, see them as chances for growth, and devise successful coping mechanisms.

Good thinking can have a good impact on both our mental and physical well-being. Studies have found a link between positive thinking and a stronger immune system. When we are optimistic and hopeful, our bodies are better able to combat ailments. Positive thinking can also help to lower blood pressure, reduce the risk of heart disease, and enhance sleep quality.

By adopting a positive mindset, we can improve our general well-being and lead more rewarding lives. It is crucial to understand that positive thinking does not imply dismissing negative emotions or pretending that everything is fine. Instead, it is important to acknowledge our issues while concentrating on solutions and possibilities. By having a positive attitude, we can change our lives and achieve greater pleasure and success.

The Science of Affirmations: How They Work

Affirmations are powerful tools for reprogramming our subconscious thoughts and cultivating a positive mindset. Repeating positive statements allows us to question negative beliefs and replace them with empowered concepts.

The power of words is undeniable. Language changes our vision of reality and influences our ideas, emotions, and actions. Positive affirmations are fundamentally a sort of self-hypnosis. Repeating these phrases creates neuronal connections in the brain that reinforce beneficial ideas.

The neurology of affirmations is intriguing. When we repeat positive sentences, our brain releases neurotransmitters such as dopamine and serotonin, which promote emotions of happiness and well-being. These neurotransmitters boost the brain's reward center, reinforcing pleasant associations with affirmations. As we repeat affirmations over time, our neural pathways strengthen, making it simpler to think positively and feel good.

The value of repetition in affirmation practice cannot be emphasized. The more we repeat our affirmations, the more deeply they penetrate our subconscious thoughts. Affirmations should be repeated every day, preferably several times per day. You can speak them aloud, write them down, or record yourself saying them.

Incorporating affirmations into our daily routine can result in a dramatic transformation in our thinking and view of life. They can help us overcome self-doubt, increase our self-esteem, and achieve our objectives. So, let us embrace the power of affirmations and begin transforming our lives today.

Creating Strong Affirmations: A Practical Guide

To generate successful affirmations, utilize positive language that speaks to you. Avoid using negative words like "not" or "don't," as your subconscious mind may interpret them incorrectly. Instead, concentrate on positive comments that affirm your desires.

For example, instead of saying "I will not be stressed," say "I am calm and peaceful." This positive affirmation emphasizes the desirable outcome rather than the negative experience you wish to avoid.

When writing affirmations, it is also beneficial to use the present tense. This helps to train your brain to believe that you already have the attributes or experiences you want. For example, instead of stating "I will be happy," say "I am happy." Using the present tense communicates to your subconscious mind that happiness is your current reality.

Personalizing your affirmations is another key consideration. The more personal and detailed your affirmations are, the more effective they will be. Instead of utilizing generic affirmations, personalize them to your specific aims and aspirations. For example, if you want to boost your self-esteem, write an affirmation like "I am confident in my abilities and believe in myself."

Here are some frequent affirmation themes that will encourage you:

Self-love and self-importance: "I love and accept myself unconditionally," "I am worthy of love and happiness," "I am confident and capable."

Abundance and prosperity: "I am financially abundant," "I attract wealth and prosperity," "I am grateful for all that I have."

Wellness and medical conditions: "I am healthy and strong." "I have boundless energy," "I nourish my body with healthy food."

Marriage and affection: "I attract loving and supportive relationships," "I am loved and cherished," "I communicate with love and kindness."

Remember that the key to making effective affirmations is to use phrases that speak to you on a deep level. When you establish a strong connection with your affirmations, they will have a greater impact on your subconscious mind.

Visualizing Success: The Power of Positive Imagery

Visualization, also known as mental imagery, is a powerful technique in which you create vivid mental images of your intended objectives. By using your imagination, you can access the power of your subconscious mind and realize your dreams.

When you visualize, you are programming your mind to succeed. Your brain cannot distinguish between real and imagined events, so when you envision a favorable conclusion, your mind begins to believe it is attainable. This belief system then pushes you to take action and achieve your goals.

To imagine successfully, select a peaceful spot where you will not be interrupted. Close your eyes and envision your desired outcome. Make use of all of your senses to create the most vivid visualization possible. Imagine yourself attaining your objective, hearing the sounds that go with it, feeling the feelings of achievement, and even smelling the aromas of your desired reality.

Regular visualization practice can result in a variety of benefits, including:

1. **Improved performance:** Visualizing oneself successful can help you improve your performance in many areas of your life, including athletics, academics, and business.
2. **Increased motivation:** Visualization can boost your motivation by painting a vivid picture of your goals and the rewards that come with attaining them.
3. **Enhanced creativity:** Engaging your imagination allows you to promote imaginative thinking and come up with novel solutions to challenges.

To maximize the usefulness of visualization, consider these tips:

Select a specific aim. The more specific your visualization, the more effective it will be. Instead of imagining overall achievement, concentrate on a specific goal, such as finding a new job or finishing a project.

Use positive phrases. When envisioning, use positive language to express the intended result. Avoid using negative language, which may undermine your efforts.

Practice regularly: The more you practice visualization, the better you will get at it. Make a daily habit of envisioning your goals.

By incorporating visualization into your everyday practice, you may harness the power of your mind and realize your ambitions. So, start picturing your achievement today and watch how your life changes.

Manifesting Your Dreams: The Law of Attraction

The Law of Attraction is a universal principle that maintains that "like attracts like." In other words, you get what you focus on. Using the Law of Attraction, you may manifest your wishes and live the life you want.

To make your ideas a reality, you must first set clear intentions. What is your true desire? Spend some time reflecting on your goals and dreams, then write them down. Be as precise as possible. The more specific your intentions, the easier it will be to realize them.

Once you have established your intentions, it is time to take inspired action. An inspired action feels good and is consistent with your aims. It is critical to avoid forcing things or acting out of desperation. Instead, follow your gut and perform actions that feel natural and effortless.

Maintaining a positive perspective is essential for realizing your dreams. Concentrate on positive ideas and emotions and avoid concentrating on negative ones or anxieties. Cultivating a positive mindset increases your chances of attracting pleasant experiences and opportunities.

To avoid frequent problems such as frustration and self-doubt, use patience and persistence. Manifestation takes time, so do not be discouraged if you do not see immediate results. Be focused on your goals and trust the universe.

Remember, the Law of Attraction is a powerful tool for creating the life you want. Setting clear intentions, taking inspired action, maintaining a positive mindset, and practicing patience will help you actualize your aspirations and live a full life.

8

Chapter 8

Recognizing the Need for Professional Help

The process of recovering from narcissistic abuse is frequently laden with emotional upheaval and psychological distress. While self-help tactics and support groups can be helpful, receiving professional treatment from a trained therapist can greatly speed up the recovery process. Recognizing the indications of emotional discomfort and the impact of narcissistic abuse on mental health is the first step toward getting the help you require.

Persistent feelings of melancholy, worry, or hopelessness are common indicators of emotional distress. These emotions may be accompanied by changes in sleep habits, appetite, and energy levels. Difficulty concentrating, making judgments, or losing interest in formerly enjoyable activities are all signs of underlying emotional anguish. For some people, increased reliance on alcohol or drugs can provide temporary relief from these overpowering emotions. In severe situations, thoughts of self-harm or suicide may emerge, emphasizing the critical need for professional help.

Narcissistic abuse can have a serious influence on mental health, causing a variety of psychological problems. Post-traumatic stress disorder (PTSD) is a prevalent diagnosis among survivors, characterized by intrusive thoughts, flashbacks, and increased alertness. Depression, marked by persistent sorrow, loss of interest, and changes in diet and sleep patterns, is another common outcome of narcissistic abuse. Anxiety disorders, such as generalized anxiety disorder and panic disorder, can also develop as a result of continuous stress and terror in an abusive relationship.

Complex post-traumatic stress disorder (C-PTSD) is a more complex type of trauma that is frequently caused by extended or recurrent exposure to stressful experiences, such as narcissistic abuse. C-PTSD is characterized by a variety of symptoms, including emotional dysregulation, relational difficulties, and a skewed sense of self. Dissociative disorders, such as depersonalization and derealization, can also emerge as coping mechanisms for people who have been through significant trauma.

Recognizing these indications of emotional distress as well as the consequences of narcissistic abuse on mental health is critical for finding proper treatment. Individuals can begin a journey of healing and rehabilitation by admitting they need professional help.

Find a Qualified Therapist

Once you have acknowledged the need for professional assistance, the next step is to identify a qualified therapist who can offer you the support and direction you require. Various types of mental health specialists can assist, each with their specialty.

Psychologists are experts on human behavior and mental processes. They are trained to assess and diagnose mental problems, as well as to provide therapy to assist patients in overcoming their challenges.

Psychiatrists are medical practitioners who focus on mental health. They can diagnose and treat mental illnesses, including with medication.

Licensed clinical social workers (LCSWs) are trained to offer therapy and counseling services. They frequently assist people and families in handling a variety of concerns, such as trauma, loss, and interpersonal difficulties.

Licensed Marriage and Family Therapists (LMFTs) work with individuals and families to strengthen their relationships. They can offer treatment to couples, families, and individuals.

When selecting a therapist, it is critical to evaluate their credentials and expertise. Look for a therapist who has worked with survivors of narcissistic abuse. It is also critical to select a therapist with whom you feel comfortable and protected. You should be able to trust your therapist and feel comfortable telling them about your experiences.

There are various approaches to finding a qualified therapist. You can ask your primary care physician for a referral. Your doctor may be able to recommend a therapist who understands your medical history and can offer you the care you require.

Another alternative is to do an online search for therapists in your region. Many therapists have websites where you can learn more about their backgrounds and experiences. You can also read reviews from previous clients to get an idea of how satisfied they were with the therapist's services.

Once you have chosen a few suitable therapists, set up consultations with each of them. This allows you to meet with the therapist and ask questions. You can also express your worries and goals for therapy.

It is critical to select a therapist with whom you are comfortable and who you believe can assist you in achieving your goals. Trust your intuition and do not be scared to browse until you discover the best fit.

The Therapeutic Process

You can start the therapy process once you have located a qualified therapist. This approach will vary depending on the therapist and your personal needs, but there are certain broad phases you can anticipate.

Initial Consultation.

The first step in the therapeutic process is an introductory consultation. This session lets you discuss your issues and goals with your therapist. Your therapist will also analyze your mental health requirements and create a treatment plan that is suited to your unique scenario.

Therapy Techniques

Survivors of narcissistic abuse can benefit from a variety of treatments. Some of the most frequent strategies are:

1. **Cognitive-behavioral therapy (CBT)** enables people to identify and address problematic thought patterns and behaviors.
2. **Dialectical behavior therapy (DBT)** teaches how to manage emotions, tolerate distress, and improve relationships.
3. **Eye Movement Desensitization and Reprocessing (EMDR):** This therapy assists people in processing painful memories and reducing their emotional impact.
4. **Psychodynamic therapy** involves analyzing unconscious ideas and feelings to obtain insight into past experiences and current behaviors.

Your therapist will work with you to identify which strategies are best suited to your needs. They may also employ a variety of strategies to develop a complete therapy plan.

The Role of the Therapist

Your therapist will play a critical role in your healing process. They will create a secure and supportive environment in which you may communicate your thoughts and feelings without being judged. They will also assist you in understanding your experiences and developing effective coping skills.

Your therapist will help you overcome negative thought patterns and establish a more positive self-image. They will also help you develop self-compassion and self-care skills. Working together, you and your therapist can create a specific treatment plan to help you overcome the difficulties of narcissistic abuse.

Overcome the stigma of seeking help.

Survivors of narcissistic abuse face a significant barrier in overcoming the stigma associated with getting help. Many people assume that seeking therapy is a sign of weakness and that they should be able to solve their problems. However, this is a hazardous myth.

Seeking therapy indicates strength, not weakness. It takes guts to admit you need help and take action to enhance your mental health. By pursuing treatment, you are investing in your health and gaining control of your life.

It is vital to know that you are not alone. Millions of people seek therapy each year, and many of them have had struggles comparable to yours. Sharing your experiences with others can help to reduce the stigma associated with seeking assistance.

Here are some suggestions for overcoming the stigma of receiving help:

Share your experiences with your valued friends and family. Talking with individuals you trust can make you feel less alone and more supported.

Join a support group. Support groups offer a safe and friendly atmosphere in which to connect with other survivors of narcissistic abuse.

Advocate for Mental Health Awareness: Sharing your story can help raise awareness about the importance of mental health while also reducing the stigma associated with seeking assistance.

Remember, getting treatment is a positive step toward healing and recovery. Do not let the stigma of requesting help prevent you from receiving the assistance you require.

Creating a Strong Therapist-Client Relationship

A strong therapist–client relationship is required for effective therapy. This connection is based on trust, respect, and open communication.

Trust and rapport

Trust is the cornerstone of all therapeutic relationships. To create trust, you must feel safe and comfortable with your therapist. You should be allowed to express your opinions and feelings without fear of being judged or criticized.

To build trust, you can:

Be upfront and honest with your therapist. Share your thoughts, emotions, and experiences, no matter how painful or embarrassing they are.

Attend regular therapy sessions: Regular participation demonstrates your dedication to the therapy process.

Actively Participate in Therapy: Discuss your views and opinions, ask questions, and finish any homework projects.

Set realistic expectations. Understand that therapy requires time and effort. Do not expect immediate results.

Effective communication

Effective communication is essential for developing a healthy therapeutic connection. To successfully interact with your therapist, you should:

Express your opinions and feelings openly. Do not be hesitant to share your thoughts.

Ask questions and get clarity. If you do not understand something, please ask for an explanation.

Give feedback on your therapy experience. Tell your therapist what is working and what is not.

Collaboration

A strong therapist-client relationship is collaborative. You and your therapist should collaborate to create a treatment plan that is personalized to your unique needs. You should also be part of the decision-making process and feel empowered to play an active role in your recovery.

Building a solid therapeutic relationship increases your chances of success in therapy.

9

Chapter 9

Assessing Your Financial Situation

The route to financial independence begins with a thorough awareness of your existing financial situation. This includes assessing your assets and obligations, determining your income and expenses, and identifying opportunities for improvement in your financial health.

Taking stock of your assets

Your assets are the resources you hold that have value. These may include cash, investments, real estate, and personal property. Understanding the worth of your assets will provide you with a better view of your overall financial status.

Cash and cash equivalents: This comprises cash in checking and savings accounts, as well as other highly liquid assets like certificates of deposit (CDs) and money market funds.

Investments: This category includes a wide variety of investment instruments such as equities, bonds, mutual funds, exchange-traded funds, and retirement accounts. It is critical to evaluate the performance of your investments and rebalance your portfolio as necessary.

Real estate holdings, including your home residence and investment properties, can be valuable assets. Consider the equity in your home and the possibilities for rental income from investment properties.

Personal possessions: Personal things such as jewelry, paintings, and collectibles may hold sentimental value, but they can also be valuable assets. Evaluate these things to establish their fair market worth.

Identify Your Liabilities

Liabilities, on the other hand, reflect your financial commitments. These debts include credit card balances, student loans, automobile loans, and mortgages. Understanding your obligations allows you to establish a strategy for managing and reducing them.

Credit Card Debt: High-interest credit card debt can rapidly get out of control. Pay off debts as soon as possible to reduce interest costs. Student loans can be a considerable burden, especially for new graduates. Consider repayment choices that include income-driven repayment plans and loan forgiveness programs.

Auto loans can be a major expense, particularly for new vehicles. Consider financing choices with cheaper interest rates and shorter loan periods.

Mortgages: Your mortgage is probably your highest loan. While this is a long-term commitment, it is critical to make on-time payments and consider refinancing to minimize your interest rate.

A thorough inventory of your assets and obligations will provide you with a clear image of your net worth. To calculate your net worth, remove your liabilities from your assets. A positive net worth implies financial health, whereas a negative net worth signifies that you should take action to improve your financial status.

Developing a Financial Plan

Once you have a clear picture of your present financial condition, the following stage is to develop a comprehensive financial strategy. A well-crafted financial plan will assist you in setting and achieving your financial objectives, efficiently managing your money, and creating a secure financial future.

Setting clear financial goals.

The first stage in developing a financial plan is to establish specific financial goals. These objectives should be specified, measurable, attainable, relevant, and time-bound (SMART). Some frequent financial goals are:

- Short-term goals:
- Create an emergency fund.
- Paying off high-interest loans.
- Saving for a vacation or a big buy.
- Long-term objectives:
- Buying a house
- Saving for retirement.
- Supporting your children's education

Setting clear goals helps keep you motivated and focused on your financial objectives.

Create a realistic budget.

A budget is a financial plan that lays out your income and expenses. Tracking your income and expenses allows you to identify areas where you may decrease costs and save more money. A well-planned budget can help you:

Monitor your spending: Monitoring your expenses allows you to identify areas where you might be overspending.

Prioritize your spending. Allocate your money to necessary expenses like housing, food, and transportation.

Save for your ambitions. Set aside some of your salary for savings and investments.

Reduce debt: Allocate funds to repay high-interest loans.

Budgeting tools like spreadsheets and apps can help you construct a realistic budget. These tools can assist you in tracking your income and expenses, establishing financial goals, and monitoring your success.

Prioritizing Financial Goals

Once you have established your financial goals, you must prioritize them. Prioritize your goals based on the following factors:

Timeframe: Prioritize short-term aims above long-term ambitions.

Importance: Prioritize goals that are critical to your financial stability.

Impact: Consider how accomplishing each goal will affect your overall financial status.

Prioritizing your goals allows you to better allocate your resources and make progress toward your financial objectives.

Create an Emergency Fund

An emergency fund serves as a safety net, allowing you to weather unanticipated financial storms. It is an essential part of a strong financial plan.

Understanding the importance of emergency funds

Life is full of uncertainty, and unexpected bills might occur at any time. An emergency fund can help you escape financial hardship and debt. Some popular reasons to use your emergency savings include:

1. **Job Loss:** If you lose your job, an emergency fund might help you get by until you locate another one.
2. **Medical Emergencies:** Unexpected medical expenses might quickly deplete your funds.
3. **Home Repairs:** Major house repairs, such as a leaking roof or a malfunctioning appliance, can be expensive.
4. **Car repairs:** Vehicle breakdowns may be inconvenient and costly.

Determining the Right Amount to Save

The amount you should set aside for an emergency fund is determined by your specific situation. A frequent guideline is to save three to six months of living expenses. This amount varies according to your income, job stability, and family size.

To decide the appropriate amount for your emergency fund, consider the following:

1. **Monthly Expenses:** Calculate your monthly expenses, such as accom-

modation, food, transportation, and utilities.

2. **Job security:** If you have a steady job with minimal danger of layoff, you may require a smaller emergency fund.

3. **Health Insurance Coverage:** If you have comprehensive health insurance, you may just need a little emergency fund.

4. **Debt obligations:** If you have a large amount of debt, you may require a larger emergency fund to pay unforeseen bills.

Strategies to build an emergency fund

Although building an emergency fund is difficult, there are many ways to do so.

1. **Automate Your Savings:** Create automatic transfers from your checking account to your savings account.

2. **Prioritize savings.** Treat your emergency money as a non-negotiable expense.

3. **Use a high-yield savings account:** Selecting a high-yield savings account will help you maximize your money.

4. **Cut back on unneeded costs.** Identify areas where you may minimize costs, such as dining out, entertainment, and subscriptions.

5. **Sell your unused items:** Sell goods you no longer need to earn extra money.

By constantly saving and investing in your emergency fund, you may shield yourself from financial difficulty and achieve financial security.

Invest in Yourself

Investing in yourself is one of the most beneficial investments you can make. By learning new skills, knowledge, and experiences, you may boost your earning potential, develop your profession, and improve your entire quality of life.

Identify your skills and talents.

The first step in investing in yourself is recognizing your abilities and qualities. Take some time to consider your talents, limitations, and hobbies. Consider these questions:

- What are your inherent abilities?
- What do you enjoy doing?
- What are your professional goals?

Once you have a better understanding of your skills and abilities, you may begin to identify areas for improvement.

Continuing education and training.

Continuing education and training can help you keep up with industry trends and learn new skills. There are numerous opportunities for continuing education, including:

- **Online Courses:** Online courses provide flexibility and convenience.
- **In-person courses:** In-person classes provide for hands-on learning and networking.

Workshops and seminars can teach you new skills and practices.

Mentorship programs offer direction and support from experienced professionals.

Networking and building relationships.

Networking is an effective tool for career growth. Building excellent relationships with other professionals can help you identify new possibilities, learn from others, and seek guidance. Here are some suggestions for networking:

1. Attend industry events. Conferences, trade exhibitions, and industry events are excellent opportunities to meet new individuals.
2. Join a professional organization: Professional groups can help you meet like-minded people.
3. Leverage social media: Connect with industry professionals through social media networks such as LinkedIn.
4. Offer assistance to others: Helping others is an excellent approach to developing relationships.

Investing in yourself allows you to realize your full potential and achieve your career objectives.

Achieve Financial Freedom

Many people consider financial freedom to be their ultimate objective. It is the condition of having enough money to live well without relying on a typical employment or paycheck. To obtain financial freedom, you must practice disciplined money management and make sound financial judgments.

Minimizing Debt

Debt can be a huge barrier to financial freedom. To reduce debt, try the following options.

Create a debt repayment plan. Prioritize high-interest debts and set aside a percentage of your salary to pay them off.

Consolidate debt: Consider combining several loans into a single one with a cheaper interest rate.

Negotiate with creditors: If you are having trouble making payments, ask your creditors to lower your interest rate or prolong your repayment period.

Maximizing Income

Consider increasing your income to help you get closer to financial freedom. Here are a few strategies:

Seek promotion or raises: Discuss your professional goals with your boss, and work hard to win promotions and raises.

Begin a side hustle: Investigate alternatives for extra income through free-lancing, consulting, or launching a small business.

Invest in rental properties. Real estate investing can result in both passive income and long-term wealth creation.

Invest in dividend-paying equities: Dividend stocks can give both regular income and capital gains.

Practice Financial Discipline

Financial discipline is essential to reaching financial freedom. Here are some ways to practice financial discipline:

Avoid making spontaneous purchases. Before you make a purchase, consider whether it is a need or a want.

Live below your means. Do not spend more than you make.

Regularly examine and adapt your financial plan. As your financial condition changes, you should examine and adjust your financial plan accordingly.

You can attain financial freedom and live an abundant life by implementing these tactics and remaining devoted to your financial goals.

Chapter 10

Embracing Your New Reality

The road to recovering your power and healing from narcissistic abuse is tremendous. It demands courage, resilience, and a strong commitment to self-love. As you embark on this transformative journey, you must embrace your new reality. This entails accepting the past, letting go of the pain, and recognizing your power.

Reflecting on your previous interactions with a narcissist can be both unpleasant and enlightening. It is critical to recognize the emotional and psychological toll that this poisonous relationship has imposed on you. However, it is critical to avoid focusing on the unpleasant aspects of the past. Instead, focus on the lessons you have learned and the progress you have made.

Letting go of the grief caused by narcissistic abuse is a difficult but necessary step in your healing process. This entails releasing negative emotions like wrath, bitterness, and sadness. Forgiveness is a helpful approach to letting go of these emotions. Forgiveness does not imply accepting the abuser's actions; rather, it involves freeing oneself from the emotional load of the past. By forgiving, you break free from the bonds of bitterness and hatred, allowing you to go forward with a lighter heart.

You must acknowledge your strength and resilience as you recover and progress. You have been through incredible agony and hardship, yet you have come out stronger than ever. Take satisfaction in your accomplishments, large and small. Recognize and celebrate your accomplishments, no matter how little they may appear. Recognizing your strengths will increase your self-esteem and foster a positive self-image.

Remember that the path to healing is not linear. There will be obstacles and challenges along the way. However, if you remain devoted to your recovery and practice self-compassion, you can overcome any hurdle.

Creating A Vision for Your Future

This new chapter in your life requires you to imagine your ideal future. Setting intentions, establishing a vision board, and breaking down your goals can help you realize your aspirations and live a life full of joy, purpose, and fulfillment.

Setting intentions entails identifying your aims and dreams. What do you want to achieve? What kind of person do you hope to become? What kind of life do you hope for? Making the effort to establish your intentions can give you a better feeling of direction and purpose. Remember to set short-term and long-term goals. Short-term objectives can help you stay motivated and track your progress, and long-term goals can give you a sense of overall direction.

Creating a vision board is an effective way to visualize your perfect existence. Gather images, quotations, and affirmations that reflect your goals. Arrange these materials on a board or digital canvas to form a visual depiction of your dreams. Regularly reviewing your vision board can reinforce your intentions and drive you to take action.

Breaking down your goals into smaller, more manageable steps can make them appear less onerous. Instead of focusing on the ultimate objective, consider the actions you must take to get there. Breaking down your goals into smaller, more doable activities will help you feel more empowered and motivated to take action.

Remember that your vision for the future is continuously shifting. As you mature and change, your goals and desires may fluctuate. Do not be scared to change your vision as needed. Flexibility and adaptation are essential for reaching your dreams.

Taking Action: Making Your Dreams a Reality

Following your clear vision of the future, take action to achieve your goals. Overcoming fear and doubt, adopting a growth mentality, and gaining momentum are all critical elements in this process.

Fear and doubt can be formidable hurdles to our growth. However, by confronting these emotions and developing self-confidence, you may conquer them. Positive self-talk is an excellent approach for increasing confidence. Instead of focusing on your limits, concentrate on your strengths and skills. Remind yourself of your previous accomplishments and trials.

A growth mentality is vital for accomplishing your objectives. Rather than perceiving issues as hurdles, see them as opportunities for growth and learning. When faced with a setback, do not give up. Instead, view these events as stepping stones to further success. By fostering a growth mentality, you will gain the resilience and determination required to overcome any problem.

Building momentum entails taking tiny, consistent moves toward your goals. Do not strive to accomplish everything at once. Instead, take one modest step at a time. Building momentum will give you the confidence and determination to take on more difficult problems.

Remember that progress is not always linear. There will be highs and lows along the journey. Do not get discouraged if you encounter obstacles. Instead, turn these moments into chances to learn and grow. You can accomplish anything you set out to do if you stay focused, persistent, and committed to your goals.

Celebrating Your Victories and Acknowledging Your Progress

As you work toward your goals, it is critical to appreciate your accomplishments, no matter how minor they may appear. Stay motivated and optimistic by practicing gratitude, praising yourself, and learning from disappointments.

Gratitude entails focusing on the positive parts of your life. Taking time each day to concentrate on what you are grateful for might help you adjust your perspective and create a more optimistic mindset. Gratitude can also help you manage stress, enhance your mood, and deepen your relationships.

Rewarding yourself for your accomplishments is another effective strategy to stay motivated. When you hit a milestone, take some time to celebrate your accomplishments. Rewarding yourself, whether it is with a special treat, a relaxing bath, or time spent with loved ones, will help you stay motivated and focused on your goals.

Setbacks are a normal aspect of life. Instead of concentrating on your setbacks, see them as opportunities to learn and progress. Analyzing what went wrong and identifying areas for improvement will help you avoid future mistakes and boost your chances of success.

Remember that success does not come easily. There will be problems and barriers on the way. However, by remaining positive, celebrating your triumphs, and learning from your failures, you can overcome any obstacle and realize your goals.

Living a Life of Purpose: Finding Meaning and Fulfillment

Finding meaning and fulfillment in life is a fundamental human goal. You may live a purposeful and joyful life by pursuing your hobbies, giving back to others, and practicing mindfulness.

Discovering your passions entails investigating your interests and abilities. What activities give you joy and satisfaction? What are you naturally talented at? Identifying your hobbies allows you to find methods to incorporate them into your everyday life. Following your passions, whether through a pastime, volunteer work, or starting a business, can lead to a more fulfilling and meaningful existence.

Giving back to others is another effective method to discover purpose. You can change the world by volunteering or donating to a cause. Helping others can boost your mood and well-being.

Mindfulness entails paying attention to the present moment without passing judgment. Mindfulness can help you reduce stress, focus better, and improve your overall quality of life. Mindfulness practices like meditation and yoga can help you connect with your inner self and live a more meaningful life.

Remember that finding purpose and contentment is a personal path. What one person finds meaningful may not be meaningful to another. You can find your way to a meaningful and rewarding life by following your passions, giving back to others, and practicing mindfulness.

11

The Journey To Healing

Acknowledging the Hurt

The path to healing begins with a deep recognition of the harm caused by narcissistic and toxic manipulation. This recognition is the first step toward release, a critical moment in which the victim moves from denial and uncertainty to clarity and empowerment. It is a tough process, frequently riddled with emotional anguish, but it is necessary for the healing to begin.

The agony caused by narcissistic abuse is both profound and subtle. It creeps into one's inner core, undermining self-esteem, shattering confidence, and leaving long-term emotional scars. The victim may experience a wide range of emotions, including anger, despair, perplexity, and disbelief. Survivors frequently question their sanity, their perceptions of reality, and whether they are to blame for the abuse.

Validating one's emotions is an important stage in the healing process. It entails admitting the validity of one's emotions and refusing to downplay or disregard them. The victim needs to learn to trust their instincts and believe in their own experiences. This can be a difficult process because the narcissist frequently gaslights his victims, making them question their reality. However, by seeking help from trusted friends, family, or a therapist, the victim can begin to validate their own experiences and restore their sense of identity.

Another essential part of the healing process is letting go of guilt and shame. Narcissists frequently blame their victims for their abusive behaviors, making the victim feel responsible for the abuse. It is critical to remember that the victim is not responsible for the narcissist's conduct. The narcissist is completely responsible for their actions, and the victim should not bear the burden of guilt or shame.

Accepting self-compassion is crucial for healing. This includes treating oneself with care, empathy, and patience. Healing takes time, and there will be obstacles along the road. Self-compassion enables the sufferer to avoid self-criticism and negative self-talk. Instead, they can prioritize self-care and self-love.

Setting boundaries and limits is an important step toward protecting oneself from additional harm. This entails setting clear limits with the narcissist and continuously maintaining them. It may be necessary to minimize or altogether discontinue communication. Setting boundaries allows the victim to regain control of their life while also protecting their mental well-being.

The impact of narcissistic abuse.

Understanding the nature of narcissistic abuse is critical to the recovery process. Narcissistic personality disorder is a mental illness marked by an exaggerated feeling of self-importance, a desire for praise, and a lack of empathy. Narcissists frequently manipulate and use people to protect their fragile egos.

Recognizing the symptoms of narcissistic abuse can be difficult since narcissists are good at concealing their true motives. However, several frequent red signals might help you recognize a poisonous relationship. These include gaslighting, love bombing, triangulation, and the silent treatment. Gaslighting is a psychological manipulation technique in which the narcissist contradicts the victim's reality, causing them to question their sanity. Love bombing is a method that involves overwhelming the victim with attention and affection, only to withhold it later as a kind of punishment. Triangulation pits the victim against others, such as friends or relatives. Silent treatment is a type of emotional abuse in which the narcissist withholds affection and communication as a means of control.

The psychological consequences of narcissistic abuse can be severe. Victims may have symptoms of post-traumatic stress disorder (PTSD), including anxiety, depression, and problems sleeping. They may also experience low self-esteem, feelings of worthlessness, and difficulties trusting people. In severe circumstances, narcissistic abuse can result in substance abuse, self-harm, or suicide.

Breaking the cycle of silence is a brave move that can help survivors of narcissistic abuse. For far too long, victims have suffered in silence, scared to speak up about their experiences. However, by sharing their tales, survivors can assist others who are going through similar circumstances. It is critical to realize that you are not alone, and others care about you and want to assist.

The value of self-preservation cannot be emphasized. Survivors can protect themselves from future damage by putting their own needs and well-being first. This may entail setting boundaries, restricting contact with the narcissist, and getting help from trusted friends, family, or a therapist. It is also critical to practice self-care, which includes spending time in nature, participating in hobbies, and getting enough sleep.

Survivors can recover their power and rebuild their lives by comprehending the impact of narcissistic abuse and taking action to heal.

Recovering Your True Self

Unmasking the fake self, which is typically created to placate the narcissist, is an important step in the recovery process. This false self, a distorted image of the genuine self, is frequently associated with self-doubt, people-pleasing, and a lack of assertiveness. By closing this false persona, survivors can begin to reconnect with their true selves.

Rebuilding self-esteem is critical to the healing process. Narcissistic abuse can destroy a person's self-esteem, leaving the victim feeling worthless and incompetent. By confronting negative self-talk and concentrating on one's qualities and successes, survivors can start to rebuild their self-esteem. It is critical to set realistic goals and appreciate small accomplishments, no matter how minor they may appear.

Cultivating self-love is an effective therapeutic strategy. Survivors of narcissistic abuse can begin to heal their wounds by practicing self-compassion and self-acceptance. This could include spending time in nature, engaging in hobbies, or simply relaxing and recharging. It is also critical to surround oneself with good and helpful people who inspire and motivate.

Accepting one's strengths and faults is a vital step in the healing process. Survivors can establish a more realistic and balanced self-image by accepting their limits while also celebrating their virtues. It is critical to avoid comparing oneself to others and instead focus on own growth and development.

Letting go of people-pleasing is an important step in the healing process. People-pleasers frequently put others' needs and desires ahead of their own. Setting boundaries and prioritizing one's well-being allows survivors to break away from the cycle of people-pleasing and live a more authentic life. It is critical to state one's demands and desires assertively and to decline when necessary.

Managing Trauma and Pain

Understanding the trauma response is critical to healing. Chronic stress and trauma cause dysregulation of the body's stress response system. This can result in a wide range of physical and emotional symptoms, including anxiety, despair, and problems sleeping. Survivors can create effective coping techniques by learning how their bodies respond to trauma.

Mindfulness and meditation can be great healing aids. These techniques can assist in calming the mind, relieve stress, and promote relaxation. By focusing on the present moment, survivors can improve their ability to manage their thoughts and emotions.

Seeking professional aid is a vital part of the recovery process. A therapist can offer survivors direction, support, and resources to help them deal with the emotional and psychological effects of narcissistic abuse. Therapy can also help survivors establish healthy coping methods and strengthen their interpersonal relationships.

Building resilience is critical for long-term healing. Survivors can boost their resilience to stress and hardship by establishing coping skills like writing, exercising, and spending time outside. It is critical to prioritize self-care and avoid harmful coping techniques like substance addiction or excessive use of social media.

Finding support and community can be quite important to healing. Connecting with others who have been through similar traumas can bring a sense of belonging and understanding. Support groups, online forums, and social media groups can be quite useful for survivors. It is critical to surround oneself with good and supporting individuals who can provide encouragement and understanding.

Breaking Free of the Cycle

Recognizing patterns of behavior is critical to breaking free from the cycle of narcissistic abuse. Identifying repeating themes and dynamics might help survivors understand the narcissist's deceptive methods. This awareness will enable them to defend themselves from future injury.

Setting healthy boundaries is critical to breaking free from the pattern of narcissistic abuse. Survivors can preserve their emotional and physical health by setting clear boundaries and regularly enforcing them. It is critical to explain one's boundaries clearly and assertively, without offering excuses or defending one's actions.

Learning to say no is an effective way to break free from the pattern of narcissistic abuse. People-pleasers frequently struggle to say no, fearing rejection and confrontation. Survivors who practice saying no can restore their control and prioritize their own needs. It is critical to be aggressive and resist apologizing for one's actions.

Letting go of control is an important step in the healing process. Narcissists frequently attempt to manipulate their victims, making them feel powerless and helpless. Accepting that one cannot control others allows survivors to restore a sense of autonomy and empowerment. It is critical to focus on what one can control, such as one's ideas, feelings, and behaviors.

Assertiveness is necessary for breaking free from the cycle of narcissistic abuse. To minimize misunderstandings and confrontation, survivors should communicate their needs and goals simply and directly. To communicate one's feelings without blaming or accusing others, utilize "I" words.

12

Chapter 2

Unmasking the False Self

Narcissistic abuse frequently results in the creation of a meticulously built veneer known as the false self. It is a skewed version of oneself created to fit the demands and expectations of a toxic person. Years of wearing this mask can make it feel like the only true identity. However, it is critical to recognize the illusion and go on a road of self-discovery.

To begin unmasking the false self, one must first recognize its presence. Confronting the narcissist's deep-seated traumas can be a tough process. It demands honesty, guts, and a willingness to confront the reality. By recognizing the mask, we may start peeling it away layer by layer.

Understanding the effects of the false self is critical. It has far-reaching implications that touch all aspects of our existence. It can cause feelings of emptiness, worthlessness, and an ongoing desire for validation. It can also make it difficult to build meaningful connections with others since we are afraid of revealing our actual selves.

To remove the mask, we must first develop self-compassion. This entails treating oneself with kindness and empathy instead of self-criticism. It entails forgiving ourselves for previous sins and accepting our flaws. By cultivating self-compassion, we may create a safe environment for healing and growth.

Meditation and mindfulness activities can also help uncover the false self. Focusing on the present moment allows us to become more aware of our thoughts and feelings. This can assist us in recognizing the thought patterns that perpetuate the false self.

As we continue to peel back the layers of the false self, we may find resistance. This is a natural aspect of the healing process. It is critical to be patient with ourselves and to recognize even minor victories. With patience and perseverance, we can restore our genuine identity and live a more authentic existence.

Rebuilding self-esteem

Rebuilding self-esteem from narcissistic abuse needs time, perseverance, and self-compassion. It is the process of recovering one's worth and realizing one's natural value.

One of the first stages toward regaining self-esteem is to question negative beliefs. Narcissistic abusers frequently utilize strategies to undermine their victims' self-esteem, sowing seeds of doubt and uncertainty. It is critical to recognize negative ideas and replace them with positive affirmations. Instead of thinking, "I am not good enough," one can say, "I am capable and worthy of love and respect."

Self-affirmation is an effective method for increasing self-esteem. Repeating positive remarks about ourselves can help reprogram our brains to think more favorably. These affirmations might be as simple as "I am strong," "I am resilient," or "I am deserving of happiness." It is critical to deliver these affirmations with conviction and belief.

Setting realistic goals is another helpful method for regaining self-esteem. By breaking down huge tasks into smaller, more manageable steps, we can gain momentum and feel accomplished. It is critical to celebrate every milestone, no matter how minor. This strengthens our confidence in our talents and motivates us to keep working toward our goals.

Celebrating accomplishments, both large and small, is critical for increasing self-esteem. By acknowledging our accomplishments, we may move our attention away from our shortcomings and onto our strengths. This can boost our confidence and capabilities.

Remember that improving self-esteem is a gradual process. It is critical to be patient with oneself and avoid comparing one's progress to others. By practicing self-compassion, confronting negative ideas, setting realistic objectives, and recognizing successes, we can gradually rebuild our self-esteem and emerge stronger than before.

Cultivating Self-Love

Cultivating self-love is an essential part of recovering from narcissistic abuse. It entails nourishing oneself, cultivating self-compassion, and accepting one's flaws. By putting self-love first, we can break free from the cycle of self-doubt and self-criticism.

Prioritizing self-care is critical for developing self-love. This entails making time for activities that benefit the mind, body, and soul. These hobbies could include spending time in nature, doing yoga or meditation, reading, or simply relaxing with a favorite book. Making self-care a priority can help us reduce stress, enhance our overall health, and boost our self-esteem.

Self-compassion is another essential component of self-love. This includes treating oneself with care, understanding, and forgiveness. Make mistakes with compassion and learn from them instead of beating ourselves up. By practicing self-compassion, we can foster a more positive and helpful internal conversation.

Accepting flaws is an essential component of self-love. It's crucial to accept that mistakes happen and no one is perfect. By admitting our flaws, we can relieve ourselves of the incessant pressure to be flawless. This can make us feel more secure and real.

Surrounding oneself with positive influences is also beneficial in developing self-love. Spending time with encouraging and motivating people might make us feel more optimistic and motivated. It is critical to avoid toxic connections and seek out those who truly care about our well-being.

We can create a deep and lasting love for ourselves by prioritizing self-care, practicing self-compassion, accepting shortcomings, and surrounding ourselves with positive influences. This self-love will enable us to recover from narcissistic abuse and lead fulfilling lives.

Accepting Your Strengths and Weaknesses.

Accepting both our talents and limitations is an important step toward recovering our identity and increasing our self-confidence. It entails identifying our distinguishing characteristics, acknowledging our limitations, and leveraging our talents to overcome obstacles.

Identifying our strengths can be an effective approach to self-empowerment. Recognizing our talents, skills, and abilities allows us to acquire a better understanding of ourselves and what we can give the world. This can boost our confidence and capabilities.

Accepting our flaws is equally crucial. It is ridiculous to expect ourselves to be perfect in all aspects of our lives. Recognizing our limitations allows us to approach issues with a realistic mentality and devise solutions to overcome them. This can help us improve and learn from our mistakes.

It is an important skill to turn one's deficiencies into strengths. We can turn our deficiencies into opportunities for progress by understanding the underlying causes and adopting plans to solve them. For example, if we struggle with public speaking, we can work on our presentation skills and get feedback from others.

Building on our strengths is an effective strategy to accomplish our goals. By focusing on our areas of competence, we may boost our productivity and effectiveness. This can make us feel more successful and satisfied.

By accepting both our talents and flaws, we can gain a more balanced and realistic image of ourselves. This can help us gain self-confidence, overcome obstacles, and lead more rewarding lives.

we discuss letting go of people-pleasing, a frequent coping mechanism for those who have endured narcissistic abuse. It is a desperate endeavor to earn approval while avoiding conflict. However, this habit can be harmful to one's mental and emotional health.

Recognizing people-pleasing habits is the first step toward breaking out of this tendency. This entails paying attention to our ideas, emotions, and actions. Are we continuously looking for validation from others? Are we fearful of disappointing others? Do we put others' needs ahead of our own? By finding these tendencies, we may start to question them.

Setting limits is critical for letting go of the need to please others. This includes communicating our wants and limitations openly and assertively. It is critical to remember that it is acceptable to say no and prioritize our well-being. Setting boundaries allows us to avoid being taken advantage of while also maintaining healthy relationships.

Prioritizing our own needs is critical in breaking away from people-pleasing. This includes setting aside time for ourselves, pursuing our interests, and caring for our physical and mental well-being. Prioritizing our personal needs can boost our self-esteem and minimize stress.

Assertive communication is a crucial ability for letting go of the need to please others. This is expressing our opinions and feelings openly and immediately, without being confrontational or passive-aggressive. By communicating assertively, we may strengthen our connections and avoid misunderstandings.

Recognizing our people-pleasing tendencies, creating boundaries, prioritizing our own needs, and exercising assertive communication can help us break away from this damaging pattern and live a more true and fulfilled life.

13

Chapter 3

Understanding the Depth of the Wound

The insidious nature of narcissistic abuse frequently leaves victims perplexed and devastated. These folks' subtle manipulation, gaslighting, and emotional upheaval can have long-term consequences for one's mental and emotional health. It is critical to recognize the indicators of narcissistic abuse and comprehend the psychological toll it exacts on its victims.

Narcissists use emotional manipulation as one of their most popular strategies. They use guilt, shame, and terror to manipulate and dominate their victims. Narcissists can undermine their victim's self-esteem and sense of value by constantly shifting blame and distorting reality. This type of deception can leave victims feeling confused, lonely, and powerless.

Another pernicious strategy is gaslighting, which includes deliberately making a victim doubt their sanity. Narcissists will deny their abusive actions, distort the truth, and accuse their victims of being excessively sensitive or imaginative. This repeated gaslighting can severely undermine the victim's belief in their perceptions and judgment.

Triangulation is a typical method employed by narcissists to incite conflict and division among their victims. They may set family members, acquaintances, or coworkers against one another, isolating their victim and leaving them feeling alone and unsupported. This deception can harm relationships and undermine the victim's sense of self.

The cycle of discarding and hoovering is another symptom of narcissistic abuse. Narcissists may abruptly abandon a relationship, only to return later, promising change and love. This sporadic reinforcement can trap victims in a harmful cycle, with the hope that the relationship will improve.

Financial abuse is another method that narcissists may use to maintain control over their victims. They may limit access to funds, influence spending decisions, or even damage their victim's career. Financial dependence might make victims feel imprisoned and unable to exit the abusive relationship.

The psychological effects of narcissistic abuse can be catastrophic. Victims may have low self-esteem, anxiety, despair, or post-traumatic stress disorder (PTSD). Constant emotional turbulence and gaslighting can destroy their self-esteem and make it difficult to trust their judgment.

In severe circumstances, victims may acquire complex PTSD (C-PTSD), which is defined by chronic trauma symptoms, trouble managing emotions, and poor relationships. Dissociation, a defense mechanism that allows people to disengage from their feelings and experiences, may emerge as a strategy to cope with the overwhelming agony and stress of narcissistic abuse.

The Path to Healing

Healing from the scars left by narcissistic abuse takes time, tolerance, and self-compassion. It is critical to acknowledge that rehabilitation is possible and that with the correct resources and tactics, victims may reclaim their lives and rebuild their sense of self.

Seeking expert treatment is an important step in the recovery process. Therapists who specialize in trauma and narcissistic abuse can provide a safe and supportive environment in which to process emotions, create coping mechanisms, and work through the complicated difficulties that result from the abuse.

Self-care routines are equally vital in the healing process. Activities that promote physical and emotional well-being, such as mindfulness meditation, yoga, and physical exercise, can help reduce stress, anxiety, and sadness. A good diet, proper sleep, and creative outlets such as art, music, or writing can all improve general well-being.

Building resilience is another critical component of healing. Creating coping methods, such as deep breathing exercises, grounding techniques, and journaling, can aid in managing overwhelming emotions and reducing the impact of triggers. Practicing self-compassion, setting realistic objectives, learning to say no, and developing a solid support system can all help boost resilience and empowerment.

Processing trauma and pain is a difficult but crucial step in the healing process. Understanding the trauma response, which includes the fight, flight, freeze, and fawn responses, can help people detect and manage their reactions to triggers. Trauma-informed practices, such as EMDR (Eye Movement Desensitization and Reprocessing) and somatic experiences, can assist in processing painful memories and integrating them into a healthier narrative.

Forgiveness, while sometimes misunderstood, may be an effective tool in the healing process. It is vital to emphasize that forgiveness does not imply accepting the abuser's behavior but rather the release of resentment and hatred that can keep one back. Victims can release the burden of the past by forgiving themselves and others, allowing them to move forward with hope and optimism.

Grieving is a normal aspect of the recovery process after narcissistic abuse. Mourning the loss of the relationship, accepting the end, and moving forward with hope can be a difficult but important journey. It is critical to allow oneself to experience the agony of loss and seek help from loved ones or a professional.

Reclaim Your Power

As you begin your healing path, remember that you can reclaim your life and rebuild your sense of self. By making deliberate efforts to empower yourself, you can break free from the bonds of narcissistic abuse and embrace a better future.

Self-awareness is one of the most effective tools in your arsenal. Understanding your own talents, shortcomings, and behavioral patterns can provide you with useful insights about your wants and desires. This self-awareness will allow you to make more informed judgments and set appropriate boundaries.

Building self-confidence is another critical step toward recovering your authority. You may gradually increase your self-esteem by appreciating your accomplishments, no matter how modest, and engaging in positive self-talk. Remember that you are deserving of love, respect, and happiness.

Taking back control of your life entails making conscious decisions and taking action. Set attainable goals, prioritize your needs, and work toward your dreams. Step outside your comfort zone and try new things.

Overcoming fear and doubt might be difficult, but it is necessary for personal development. By confronting your anxieties and addressing negative beliefs, you might gain a better feeling of self-confidence. Remember that courage is not the absence of fear but the willingness to act in the face of it.

Embracing your independence is an effective strategy to recover your control. You can overcome the codependency that frequently occurs in narcissistic relationships by relying on your resources and making your own decisions.

As you begin your healing path, remember that progress takes time. Be patient with yourself and recognize your accomplishments, no matter how tiny. By taking one step at a time, you may create a brighter future and live a life full of love, peace, and purpose.

Let Go of the Past

Letting go of the past is an important step in the healing process. It permits you to let go of the burdens of the past and embrace a better future. While it can be difficult, forgiving yourself and others is necessary to move forward.

Forgiveness does not imply supporting the abuser's behavior. It is about letting go of the resentment, anger, and hurt that are holding you back. Forgiveness frees you from the emotional burden of the past, allowing you to experience love, joy, and serenity.

Self-forgiveness is equally vital. It is natural to make mistakes and face disappointments. Instead of focusing on your inadequacies, concentrate on learning from your experiences and developing as a person. Be kind to yourself and treat yourself with the same care and understanding as you would a friend.

Healing from prior relationships can be a difficult process, particularly if the relationship was poisonous or abusive. To protect your emotional health, limit or stop communicating with the narcissist. However, it is critical to examine your emotions about the relationship and let go of any residual attachment.

Releasing negative emotions like anger, resentment, and sadness is an important stage in the healing process. These feelings might weigh you down and slow your progress. Journaling, meditation, and therapy can help you learn to express and process your emotions healthily.

Moving forward with hope entails cultivating an optimistic attitude and making goals for the future. You may overcome difficulties and achieve your goals by focusing on your strengths, appreciating your accomplishments, and envisioning a greater future. Remember, hope is a powerful tool that can help you get through difficult situations.

Embracing the future requires letting go of the past and welcoming the unknown with open arms. It is about believing in yourself and your potential to lead a fulfilling life. You may achieve your full potential and live a fulfilling life by taking chances, moving outside of your comfort zone, and seizing new possibilities.

14

Chapter 4

Recognizing Patterns of Behavior

The first step toward breaking free from the cycle of narcissistic and toxic manipulation is to recognize the subtle patterns of conduct that define these relationships. By recognizing these red flags and comprehending the cyclical nature of abuse, victims can begin to unravel the complicated web of deception and reclaim their sense of self.

One of the most popular strategies used by narcissists and toxic manipulators is gaslighting. This insidious form of psychological abuse is an intentional attempt to instill doubt and uncertainty in the victim's mind, causing them to question their reality. The abuser attempts to control the narrative by dismissing the victim's experiences, diminishing their feelings, and twisting the reality.

Another common approach is manipulation, which entails utilizing a variety of strategies to control and manipulate people. Narcissists and toxic manipulators may use emotional blackmail, guilt trips, or threats to coerce their victims into obedience. They may also utilize love-bombing, a tactic that involves showering their victim with excessive attention and care to create a false sense of security before withdrawing love and support.

Another typical form of manipulation is the silent treatment, which is used to punish and control victims. By withholding affection, attention, or communication, the abuser attempts to cause fear and worry in their relationship. This strategy can be especially devastating because it makes the victim feel alienated, confused, and needy for the abuser's approval.

Understanding the cyclical nature of abuse is critical to breaking away from it. Narcissistic relationships frequently follow a predetermined pattern known as the cycle of abuse. This cycle normally comprises four stages: idealization, devaluation, discard, and hoover.

Throughout the idealization phase, the abuser lavishes the victim with attention, affection, and compliments. They may appear faultless and attentive, making the victim feel cherished and special. However, this is frequently a ruse, since the abuser's ultimate motivation is to acquire control over the victim.

Once the abuser has won the victim's confidence and affection, they will begin the devaluation phase. During this stage, the abuser starts to criticize, degrade, and undermine the victim. They may also utilize gaslighting, manipulation, and other types of emotional abuse. The victim may experience confusion, hurt, and uncertainty about their reality.

If the victim tries to confront the abuser's behavior or establish boundaries, they may enter the discard phase. During this stage, the abuser may abruptly terminate the relationship, leaving the victim feeling abandoned and dis-traught. However, the abuse cycle is not always linear, and the abuser may return to the hoover phase, promising change and affection to re-engage the victim.

Victims can begin to break away from the cycle of abuse by recognizing these patterns of conduct and comprehending their repetitive nature. It is crucial to remember that the abuser's actions do not represent the victim's worth or value. Victims can begin to heal their past wounds and establish a brighter future by getting help from friends, family, or a therapist.

Establishing Healthy Boundaries.

Setting healthy boundaries is an important step toward stopping the cycle of narcissistic and toxic manipulation. Victims can protect themselves from future trauma and restore their sense of self by setting clear boundaries and expectations.

One of the first steps in establishing healthy limits is to determine personal boundaries. These limitations may be physical, emotional, intellectual, or material. Physical boundaries involve limiting physical touch, intimacy, or proximity. Emotional boundaries are about protecting one's emotional well-being by reducing emotional commitment in unhealthy situations. Intellectual boundaries are used to shield one's thoughts, opinions, and beliefs from manipulation and control. Setting material boundaries entails limiting financial support, sharing assets, and time obligations.

Once personal limits have been established, they must be communicated clearly and assertively. This can be accomplished by using "I" statements to express one's wants and emotions without blaming or accusing the other person. For example, instead of expressing, "You always make me feel bad about myself," you may say, "I feel hurt and disrespected when you criticize me in front of others."

Setting limitations is another critical component of establishing healthy boundaries. This entails saying no to requests or demands that do not accord with one's principles or priorities. It is critical to remember that it is acceptable to say no and that doing so does not constitute a negative person.

Enforcing penalties is another important element in establishing healthy boundaries. If the abuser continues to break boundaries, it is critical to enforce the previously agreed-upon consequences. This could include limiting communication, quitting the relationship, or obtaining legal assistance.

Victims can begin to reclaim their power and control over their lives by establishing and enforcing appropriate boundaries. It is critical to remember that establishing limits is neither selfish nor unkind. It is an essential act of self-preservation. Victims can free themselves from toxic relationships, making room for good, rewarding relationships and a brighter future.

Learn to Say No

Learning to say no is an effective way to break free from the cycle of narcissistic and poisonous manipulation. It enables people to prioritize their own needs, create boundaries, and safeguard their mental health.

Fear of being disapproved of is one of the most difficult aspects of saying no. Narcissists and toxic manipulators frequently use guilt, shame, and manipulation to coerce their victims into meeting their demands. However, it is critical to remember that it is acceptable to prioritize one's own needs and decline without feeling guilty or selfish.

Overcoming the fear of rejection necessitates developing self-compassion and self-esteem. Individuals can boost their self-esteem by exercising self-care, using positive self-talk, and surrounding themselves with encouraging others. This newfound confidence will allow them to say no without fear of being judged or rejected.

Direct and honest communication is another excellent way to say no. Individuals can avoid misunderstandings and the possibility of exploitation by declaring their boundaries clearly and assertively. It is critical to employ "I" phrases to express one's emotions and demands without blaming or accusing the other person.

Offering alternatives is another effective approach for saying no. Individuals can maintain positive relationships while remaining true to their boundaries by proposing alternate ideas or concessions. For example, if someone requests to borrow money, one could offer to assist them in finding another option, such as applying for a loan or reducing costs.

Avoiding excuses is another crucial component of saying no. Individuals might avoid lengthy disputes or justifications by delivering a simple and succinct explanation. It is critical to be forceful and direct while being polite and considerate.

Individuals who master the skill of saying no can reclaim their power and have more fulfilled lives. It is a courageous deed that necessitates bravery, self-awareness, and perseverance. Individuals can break free from the cycle of narcissistic and toxic manipulation by continually setting boundaries and prioritizing their own needs, resulting in a better future.

Let Go of Control

Letting go of control is a difficult but necessary step toward breaking free from the cycle of narcissistic and poisonous manipulation. It entails understanding the illusion of control, embracing uncertainty, and believing in the process.

The illusion of control is a frequent human propensity to feel that we have complete control over our lives, including the actions of others. However, this is a mistaken perception that can result in irritation, anxiety, and disappointment. Recognizing that we cannot control everything relieves us of the burden of false expectations and the urge to micromanage every circumstance.

Accepting uncertainty is a vital part of letting go of control. Life is full of unexpected twists and turns, and attempting to control each event is foolish. By embracing uncertainty, we can increase our flexibility, resilience, and adaptability.

Trusting the process is another important aspect of letting go of control. This means accepting life's flow and trusting that it will work out. Trusting in a greater power, the universe, or our intuition allows us to let go of the desire to control and micromanage every aspect of our existence.

Practicing detachment is an effective method for letting go of control. This entails establishing emotional, physical, and mental distance from poisonous events and individuals. Emotional detachment entails learning to separate from the emotional upheaval created by narcissistic and toxic manipulation. This can be accomplished through mindfulness techniques, therapy, or just dedicating time to self-care.

Physical detachment entails establishing a physical distance between oneself and the toxic individual. This could include limiting communication, moving to a new area, or simply spending less time together. Mental detachment is releasing unpleasant ideas and ruminations about the harmful connection. This can be accomplished through meditation, journaling, or speaking with a trusted friend or therapist.

Individuals who let go of control can have a wonderful sense of liberation and calm. It is a difficult yet rewarding process that demands patience, effort, and self-compassion. Individuals who embrace uncertainty, trust the process, and practice detachment can break free from the cycle of narcissistic and toxic manipulation and live a more satisfying life.

Practice Assertiveness

Assertiveness is an essential ability for breaking free from the cycle of narcissistic and poisonous manipulation. It entails stating one's needs and desires directly, advocating for oneself, and responding positively to criticism.

Developing self-confidence is vital for assertiveness. Individuals can boost their self-esteem and confidence in their talents by practicing positive self-talk, confronting negative beliefs, and picturing success.

Positive affirmations are extremely effective strategies for increasing self-confidence. Repeating positive remarks about oneself might remodel the subconscious mind and lead to a more optimistic self-image. Like the statement: "I am strong, capable, and deserving of love and respect."

Challenging negative beliefs is another effective strategy for increasing self-confidence. Individuals who detect and challenge poor self-talk can replace self-defeating attitudes with more positive and realistic ones. Instead of thinking, "I am not good enough," one could consider, "I am learning and growing, and I am capable of achieving my goals."

Visualizing achievement is another effective method for increasing self-confidence. Individuals can motivate themselves and boost their confidence in their talents by seeing themselves achieving their goals.

Communicating assertively entails expressing one's demands and desires directly, respectfully, and effectively. This can be accomplished by using "I" statements to express one's emotions and demands without blaming or accusing the other person. For example, instead of expressing, "You always make me feel bad about myself," you may say, "I feel hurt and disrespected when you criticize me in front of others."

Standing up for oneself is a crucial part of assertiveness. This includes establishing boundaries, saying no, and arguing for one's rights. It is critical to do so calmly and assertively, without resorting to anger or defensive behavior.

Responding to criticism constructively entails listening to input with an open mind, accepting the reality of the criticism, and taking steps to improve. It is critical to avoid being defensive or assaulting the other person. Instead, focus on the message rather than the messenger.

Individuals who practice assertiveness can break free from the cycle of narcissistic and toxic manipulation and develop healthier, more rewarding relationships. It is a technique that demands practice and patience, but the benefits outweigh the effort.

15

Chapter 5

Recognizing Your Worth

The route to reclaiming power starts with a deep awareness of your intrinsic value. This is the foundation on which you will rebuild your life. For too long, you may have enabled the narcissistic manipulator to damage your self-esteem, leading you to believe that you are inadequate. It is time to destroy this false narrative and accept your genuine worth.

Begin by confronting any negative self-talk that has been imprinted in your mind. Those self-deprecating thoughts, doubts, and feelings of inadequacy do not reflect your genuine self. They are the relics of the abuse you suffered. Replace the negative thoughts with positive affirmations. Every day, remind yourself of your talents, successes, and potential.

Remember that you are a child of God, fearfully and wonderfully made (Psalm 139:14). You deserve love, respect, and happiness. Nobody, not even a narcissist, can decrease your innate worth.

Self-compassion is another valuable tool on your path to self-worth. Be gentle to yourself, especially in trying times. Treat yourself with the same love and understanding that you would extend to a close friend. Practice self-care, whether it be taking a long bath, reading a relaxing book, or simply spending time outdoors.

Celebrate your accomplishments, no matter how minor they may appear. Every step forward and every challenge overcome demonstrates your strength and resilience. Take joy in your accomplishments and let them drive your self-esteem.

As you continue to acknowledge your worth, you will gain confidence and attract wonderful individuals into your life. Remember, you deserve to be around people who encourage and support you, not those who want to dominate and manipulate you.

Establishing Healthy Boundaries.

Setting healthy limits is an important step toward recovering your control. It entails identifying acceptable and unacceptable behavior and communicating those boundaries clearly and consistently. This can be a difficult undertaking, especially if you have spent years allowing people to push your limits. However, it is crucial for your health and pleasure.

Start by identifying areas where you've let others overstep. This could involve your time, energy, emotions, or physical space. Once you have identified these locations, you may start setting constraints.

When communicating your boundaries, be direct and assertive. Avoid apologizing or offering excuses. Simply express your wants and expectations. You might say, "I need some time to myself today." I will be available to talk later." Or it may be: "I am not comfortable discussing that topic right now."

Setting and enforcing your boundaries are both crucial. Do not be scared to decline requests that do not correspond with your priorities. If someone continues to push your boundaries, do not be afraid to withdraw yourself from them.

Learning to say no can be challenging, especially if you have a tendency to please others. Remember that it is okay to prioritize your own needs. You do not need to be everything to everyone. Saying no to others means saying yes to yourself.

Setting appropriate limits also includes protecting your energy. Limit your exposure to hazardous individuals and situations. Surround yourself with good, supportive people who will encourage and inspire you.

Taking Back Control

Regaining control of your life is a significant step toward healing and empowerment. It entails identifying areas in which you have given up control, reclaiming your autonomy, and making decisions that are consistent with your values and aspirations.

Find the areas where you've let others control your life. This could be your career, relationships, or finances. Once you have recognized these locations, you may start to regain control.

Making decisions based on your wants and needs is an essential part of reclaiming your control. Do not let fear or doubt hold you back. Trust your instincts and take action.

Prioritizing your needs is critical to your well-being. Do not give up your happiness for the sake of others. Schedule time for yourself to unwind, rejuvenate, and pursue your interests.

Breaking out from codependency is another crucial step in regaining power. Codependency is a pattern of conduct in which one person relies on another for emotional and psychological support. This might cause emotions of anxiety, insecurity, and low self-esteem. Setting healthy boundaries and addressing your own needs will help you break free from codependency and live a more fulfilling life.

Increasing Self-Confidence

Developing self-confidence is a process, not a destination. It demands constant effort and self-confidence. You can gain confidence by questioning self-limiting ideas, practicing positive self-talk, and venturing beyond your comfort zone.

One of the first steps in developing self-confidence is to recognize and fight self-limiting beliefs. These are the negative beliefs and assumptions that hold you back. For example, you may believe that you are not decent enough, educated enough, or worthy of love. Recognizing these ideas allows you to begin challenging and replacing them with positive affirmations.

Positive self-talk is an effective method for increasing self-confidence. Be gentle with yourself and avoid self-criticism. Remind yourself of your talents, achievements, and potential.

Getting out of your comfort zone is another beneficial approach to boosting self-esteem. Try new things, take risks, and push yourself. Every time you face a fear or a difficulty, you acquire confidence and strength.

It is crucial to realize that setbacks are a natural part of life. Do not be discouraged by your shortcomings. Instead, view them as opportunities to learn and develop. You can develop resilience and confidence by taking on difficulties and learning from your errors.

Celebrating your accomplishments, no matter how minor, is essential for developing self-confidence. Take the time to recognize your accomplishments and thank yourself for your hard work.

Embrace Your Independence

Accepting your independence is a significant step in reclaiming your authority. It entails developing self-reliance, establishing a solid support system, and enjoying life on your terms.

Cultivating self-reliance entails accepting responsibility for your own pleasure and well-being. It entails learning to rely on oneself rather than others to meet your requirements. This could include gaining new skills, making financial objectives, or simply learning to be content with solitude.

Creating a strong support network is critical to emotional and social well-being. Surround yourself with positive, supportive others who believe in you. This could be friends, family, or members of a support group.

Financial independence is another critical component of embracing your independence. Taking charge of your finances allows you to lessen your dependency on others while increasing your sense of security.

Emotional independence refers to the ability to regulate one's own emotions without relying on others for affirmation or acceptance. This includes adopting healthy coping mechanisms like mindfulness meditation and journaling.

Living life on your terms entails making decisions that are consistent with your values and ambitions. Do not let fear or doubt hold you back. Accept your identity and live truthfully.

16

Chapter 6

Letting Go of Resentment and Anger

Resentment and fury are strong emotions that, if not controlled, can consume us. When we hold onto these emotions, they can weigh heavily on our hearts and thoughts, preventing us from going ahead and enjoying true happiness.

To let go of resentment and wrath, we must first identify the underlying causes. Past wounds and disappointments are frequently the source of these feelings. Perhaps we were wronged by someone we trusted, or we suffered a great loss. These encounters can leave profound wounds that require time to heal.

However, hanging onto these unpleasant emotions simply adds to our pain. It is like wearing a huge burden that drags us down and prevents us from realizing our greatest potential. To genuinely recover, we must learn to release the past and embrace the present.

Forgiveness is a wonderful tool for letting go of resentment and hatred. Forgiveness does not imply accepting the conduct of others; rather, it entails releasing the hurt and hatred that we hold onto. When we forgive, we break free from the bonds of the past and open ourselves to love and compassion.

Forgiving oneself is as vital as forgiving others. We all make mistakes, so we must learn without punishing ourselves. Self-compassion permits us to accept our flaws while striving for growth and change.

To practice forgiveness, we must first acknowledge our anger and resentments. Instead of denying these feelings, we might allow ourselves to experience them fully. Once we have acknowledged our emotions, we may start letting them go. This can be accomplished through a variety of methods, including journaling, meditation, or talking to a trusted friend or therapist.

Journaling can be an effective method for processing our feelings. Writing about our experiences allows us to develop a better grasp of our emotions and thoughts. Meditation can help us relax and develop a sense of tranquility. Talking to a trusted friend or therapist can offer us comfort and advice as we work through the healing process.

Remember that letting go of resentment and anger is a process, not a goal. It may need time and work, but the results are well worth it. By releasing these negative feelings, we can find more peace, joy, and fulfillment in our lives.

healing past relationships.

Healing from former relationships is an important stage in our journey of self-discovery and personal development. When we hold unresolved difficulties from previous relationships, we may find it difficult to build positive connections in the present.

To begin healing, we must first recognize the emotional consequences of these previous relationships. Honoring our sadness, disappointment, and hurt is crucial. By noticing these feelings, we may begin to process them and release the negative energy that comes with them.

One of the most important lessons from past relationships is how to recognize and overcome toxic tendencies. These tendencies may include codependency, people-pleasing, or a preference for emotionally unavailable mates. Recognizing these tendencies allows us to take action to disrupt them and foster stronger relationships in the future.

It is equally important to learn from our mistakes and failures. Mistakes are a natural part of life and can teach us important lessons. Instead of concentrating on our previous failures, we can turn them into opportunities for growth and development. Reflecting on our experiences allows us to better understand ourselves and our relationships.

Closing emotional chapters is a key step in the healing process. We can close the emotional chapters of our old relationships in the same way that we would do with physical books. This entails letting go of any remaining feelings of attachment, resentment, or wrath. By doing so, we can make room for new starts and healthier relationships.

Journaling, meditation, and talking to a therapist can all help us finish emotional chapters. Journaling allows us to communicate our ideas and emotions, whereas meditation can help us relax and achieve a sense of tranquility. A therapist can offer us tools and techniques for dealing with challenging emotions and moving ahead.

Remember that recovering from former relationships is a journey, not a race. It takes time and patience to move through the pain and envision a better future. Taking tiny actions each day allows us to progressively heal our scars and establish stronger, healthier connections.

Releasing negative emotions.

Anger, sadness, and fear are all normal human emotions. However, if these emotions go unregulated, they can cause substantial emotional and physical pain. To live a full life, it is critical to understand how to recognize and control unpleasant emotions healthily.

Identifying and acknowledging negative emotions is one of the first steps toward overcoming them. We often try to repress or dismiss our emotions, but this just leads to further issues. By admitting our feelings, we can begin to understand the underlying causes and build appropriate coping techniques.

Once we have identified our emotions, we can employ appropriate coping techniques to deal with them. Some successful coping mechanisms are:

Mindfulness and meditation: These techniques can help us relax and be more present in the moment.

Physical Activity: Exercise is an excellent strategy to reduce stress and improve mood.

Creative Outlets: Creative pursuits like painting, writing, and music can help us express our feelings healthily.

Social Connection: Spending time with loved ones can provide us strength and comfort.

Professional Help: If our emotions become overwhelming, seeing a therapist or counselor can help.

In addition to these strategies, self-compassion is essential. This entails treating ourselves with compassion and empathy, just as we would a friend. By being patient with ourselves, we can mitigate the negative effects of stress and anxiety.

Remember that removing unpleasant emotions is a continuous process. It is critical to be patient with ourselves and to recognize our accomplishments, no matter how minor they may appear. We may improve our emotional management and live a more fulfilling life by exercising healthy coping skills and fostering self-compassion.

Moving Forward with Hope.

Moving forward with hope, especially after severe trials or failures, can be intimidating. However, cultivating a positive mindset is essential for navigating life's challenges and embracing a brighter future.

Setting achievable future objectives is one of the most effective methods for building hope. Setting feasible goals allows us to break down larger ambitions into smaller, more doable tasks. This can help us stay motivated and concentrated even when confronted with challenges.

Focusing on the present moment is another important method for going forward with hope. By dwelling on the past or future, we miss out on the present. By practicing mindfulness, we can learn to enjoy the beauty of the present moment while also reducing stress and worry.

Embracing optimism and thankfulness can have a major impact on our overall well-being. By focusing on the positive things in our lives, we can change our perspective and build a more optimistic approach. Gratitude practices, such as keeping a gratitude notebook or expressing thanks to others, can help us realize the positive aspects of our lives and lessen emotions of negativity.

Remember that hope is a decision. It is a decision to believe in a better future, even when things appear grim. We may overcome obstacles and live a happier and more hopeful life by adopting a positive mindset, setting realistic goals, and practicing gratitude.

Embrace the Future

Embracing the future entails letting go of the past and facing the uncertainty with confidence and optimism. It is about developing a vision for your perfect life and taking action to make it a reality.

To begin, let go of the past and all the unpleasant emotions that come with it. Forgive yourself and others for past mistakes, and let go of resentment and wrath. We may release ourselves from the weight of the past and welcome the future with open arms.

Once we have let go of the past, we may begin to envision our perfect future. This includes establishing clear goals and purposes for our lives. What do we hope to achieve? What kind of person do we hope to become? Visualizing our preferred future might motivate us to take action and make our aspirations a reality.

Taking action is the key to realizing our dreams. This is breaking down our goals into smaller, more attainable chunks and taking consistent action toward them. It could entail getting out of our comfort zones, taking risks, and persevering through difficulties. However, the rewards for taking action are incalculable.

As we continue on our road to a greater future, we must believe in our power to create the life we want. We can overcome challenges and achieve our objectives by developing self-belief and confidence. We must remember that we are capable of amazing things and that our possibilities are infinite.

We can construct a life full of joy, fulfillment, and purpose by looking forward with hope and optimism to the future. Remember that we are empowered to affect the future and make it a better place.

17

Chapter 7

Understanding Healthy Relationships

A healthy relationship is essential for emotional well-being and general life happiness. It is a bond built on mutual respect, trust, empathy, and open communication. Such connections give a secure area for people to be themselves, express their emotions, and seek help.

Individual needs and experiences make it difficult to define beneficial partnerships objectively. However, several common features define a healthy relationship:

Mutual respect is the foundation of all healthy relationships. It entails valuing each other's perspectives, emotions, and limits. Both spouses should respect each other with kindness, consideration, and dignity.

Trust is vital for establishing intimacy and emotional stability. It entails being honest, trustworthy, and dependable. Both partners should feel safe and secure in their relationship, confident that their other would not violate their confidence.

Empathy is the ability to comprehend and share the emotions of another person. It entails placing yourself in the shoes of another person and attempting to understand the world through their eyes. This promotes stronger ties and more effective conflict resolution.

Open communication is essential for maintaining a healthy connection. It entails communicating your views, feelings, and needs honestly and politely. It also entails attentively listening to your partner's viewpoint and responding with empathy and understanding.

Recognizing the indicators of a positive relationship can be difficult, especially if you have had negative relationships in the past. Paying attention to specific indications can help you recognize healthy dynamics.

Feeling Safe and Secure: In a successful relationship, you should feel comfortable and secure with your partner. No need to worry about their reactions or physical or emotional harm.

Mutual Respect: Even when they disagree, both spouses should respect the other. They should refrain from name-calling, insults, and other forms of verbal abuse.

Open and honest communication is a defining characteristic of healthy relationships. Both partners should feel free to share their views, feelings, and needs without fear of judgment or condemnation.

Shared Values and Goals: Individual interests are vital, but shared values and goals can deepen a partnership. This can include shared hobbies, beliefs, or life goals.

Emotional intimacy is when you share your deepest thoughts, feelings, and worries with your companion. It fosters a sense of connection and understanding.

Conflict Resolution: Healthy partnerships have effective techniques to resolve disagreements. Both spouses should compromise and find mutually beneficial solutions.

Support and Encouragement: A healthy relationship entails supporting one another's aspirations and dreams. Both spouses should encourage each other's growth and development.

Comparing healthy and negative relationships might help you discover toxic relationships. Here are a few important differences:

Healthy relationships:

- **Mutual Respect:** Both partners regard each other's thoughts and emotions.
- **Trust:** Both partners are trustworthy and dependable.
- **Open Communication:** Both partners talk freely and honestly.
- **Shared values and aims:** The partners have similar values and aims.
- **Emotional Intimacy:** Both parties experience an emotional connection.
- **Conflict Resolution:** Both partners are capable of resolving disagreements peacefully.

Both partners support and encourage each other's dreams and aspirations.

Unhealthy Relationship:

- **Lack of Respect:** One or both spouses may be dismissive or disrespectful of the other's feelings.
- **Trust Issues:** One or both couples may have problems trusting the other.
- **Poor communication:** One or both partners may avoid uncomfortable

conversations or resort to blaming and accusing.

- **Incompatible values and aims:** One or both couples may have opposing values and aims.
- **Emotional Distance:** One or both spouses may experience emotional disconnection. One or both couples may have frequent disputes and conflicts.
- **Lack of Support and Encouragement:** One or both partners may be critical or dismissive of the other's dreams and goals.

Understanding the features of positive relationships and identifying the warning signs of unhealthy relationships allows you to make informed decisions about the relationships you nurture. Remember that a healthy relationship needs both effort and compromise, as well as a genuine desire to connect with someone else.

Setting Boundaries.

Setting boundaries is an important part of developing and maintaining successful relationships. Boundaries are invisible lines that define what constitutes acceptable and inappropriate behavior. They preserve our mental and physical well-being while also allowing us to accurately convey our wants and expectations.

The significance of boundaries cannot be emphasized. Without boundaries, we may find ourselves feeling overwhelmed, disgruntled, or taken advantage of. Setting and enforcing boundaries allows us to build healthy relationships based on mutual respect and understanding.

Identifying personal limits can be a difficult task. It entails self-reflection and recognizing our own needs, ideals, and limitations. Here are some questions to consider when determining your boundaries.

1. What are my core values?
2. What are my limitations in terms of time, energy, and emotional capacity?
3. Which behaviors are unacceptable to me?
4. What should I do to be respected and valued?

Once you have determined your boundaries, it is critical to convey them effectively. This includes expressing your requirements and expectations clearly and strongly. Avoid passive-aggressive rhetoric and making demands. Instead, utilize "I" expressions to describe your emotions and demands. For example, rather than saying, "You always take me for granted," you may say, "I feel hurt and undervalued when my needs are not met."

Enforcing boundaries can be challenging, especially if you are used to pleasing others or avoiding conflict. However, it is necessary to maintain healthy partnerships. When someone exceeds a boundary, it is critical to handle the situation calmly and assertively. You may need to reinforce your barrier or impose a consequence for future infractions.

Remember, setting boundaries is neither selfish nor unkind. This self-care prioritizes your needs and well-being. Setting and enforcing limits can help you build healthier, more meaningful relationships.

Effective Communication.

Effective communication is the foundation of any healthy relationship. It entails communicating our thoughts, feelings, and needs clearly and respectfully, as well as actively listening to others. When we communicate successfully, we strengthen relationships, resolve issues calmly, and promote mutual understanding.

Active listening is a powerful communication technique in which you pay full attention to the speaker without interrupting or passing judgment. It entails listening with empathy and understanding while replying thoughtfully. To practice active listening, we can employ the following techniques:

1. **Maintain eye contact**: This demonstrates your engagement and attention to what the other person is saying.
2. **Avoid distractions**: To focus on the talk, put away your phone and other distractions.
3. **Use nonverbal clues**, like nodding and smiling, to demonstrate that you are listening and understanding.
4. To ensure understanding, paraphrase what the other person stated.
5. **Ask clarifying questions:** If you are not sure about something, ask clarifying questions to help you comprehend.
6. **Avoid interrupting:** Let the other person complete speaking before reacting.
7. **Empathy** is the ability to understand another person's point of view and emotions.

Another skill required for good communication is assertiveness. It entails expressing your opinions and feelings openly and clearly, without being confrontational or passive-aggressive. Assertive communication promotes self-confidence and respect, as well as more successful conflict resolution. We can practice assertive communication using the tactics listed below:

1. **Use "I" statements,** which emphasize your own emotions and experiences rather than blaming or accusing the other person.
2. **Be specific:** Express your wants and expectations.
3. **Be direct**: Get to the point without skirting the issue.
4. **Be respectful:** Even if you disagree with someone, you may still show respect.

5. **Use nonverbal cues:** Your body language can help emphasize your message. Maintain eye contact, speak in a firm tone, and avoid crossing your arms or legs.

Body language, facial gestures, and tone of voice can all contribute significantly to efficient communication. Our nonverbal cues can frequently convey more than our words, so we must be conscious of our body language and how others perceive it. To improve your nonverbal communication, pay attention to your body language and attempt to be aware of the messages you are delivering.

Conflict resolution in a constructive manner is another crucial part of effective communication. When confrontations emerge, it is critical to address the situation with a calm and sensible attitude. Avoid blaming, accusing, or acting defensively. Instead, focus on finding a solution that benefits everyone involved. Here are some suggestions for settling conflicts constructively.

- Active listening means paying attention to the other person's point of view without interrupting them.
- Validate their feelings: Recognize the other person's emotions, even if you disagree with them.
- Use "I" phrases to express your feelings and demands without blaming or accusing.
- Find common ground: Look for points of agreement and compromise.

If you are unable to resolve the problem on your own, try seeking assistance from a mediator or counselor.

By exercising these excellent communication skills, we may strengthen our relationships, handle issues calmly, and live a more pleasant and satisfying life.

Nurturing Relationship

Maintaining connections necessitates continual effort and attention. It entails developing a sense of community, trust, and mutual respect. We can build our friendships and form long-term connections by devoting time and effort to our interactions.

Building trust is essential for every healthy connection. Trust is built over time through consistent behavior and open communication. To earn trust, you must be dependable, follow through on promises, and be open about your objectives. Avoid lying, cheating, or hiding information, as these behaviors can undermine trust and harm the relationship.

Appreciation is another crucial part of developing relationships. Expressing thanks and recognizing the positive contributions of others helps develop ties and foster a healthy environment. Small gestures like saying "thank you," giving compliments, or offering assistance can go a long way toward making others feel valued and appreciated.

Spending quality time together is critical for developing relationships. This entails setting aside specific time to connect and interact with loved ones. Quality time can deepen bonds and strengthen relationships, whether it is through a shared hobby, a heart-to-heart conversation, or simply spending time together.

Providing support and empathy is critical for developing strong relationships. When our loved ones are going through a difficult time, it is important to be there for them, whether it is by listening, offering a shoulder to cry on, or providing practical assistance. During difficult times, we can comfort and support others by demonstrating empathy and understanding.

Forgiveness is a powerful tool for strengthening relationships. Holding onto resentment and anger can harm relationships and cause distance. Forgiving others relieves us of the burden of negative emotions and opens the door to healing and reconciliation. Forgiveness does not condone harmful behavior, but rather the decision to let go of the pain and move on.

We can enrich our lives by cultivating relationships through trust, appreciation, quality time, support, empathy, and forgiveness.

Attracting Positive People.

Attracting positive people into your life requires a combination of self-love, a positive attitude, and proactive social engagement. Cultivating these qualities allows you to make meaningful connections and foster healthy relationships.

Self-love and self-worth are essential for attracting positive people. When you value yourself, you radiate confidence and attract others who appreciate your authenticity. Practice self-compassion and positive self-talk and celebrate your accomplishments, no matter how small. By embracing your individuality and recognizing your strengths, you become a magnet for positive relationships.

A positive mindset is crucial for attracting positive people. Your thoughts and beliefs shape your reality, so cultivate a positive outlook on life. Focus on gratitude, optimism, and the good in people. By radiating positivity, you attract like-minded individuals who share your optimistic perspective.

Socializing and networking are effective ways to meet new people and expand your social circle. Attend social events, join clubs or groups that align with your interests, and volunteer in your community. Engage in conversations, be open to new experiences, and actively listen to others. By putting yourself out there, you increase your chances of connecting with positive and supportive individuals.

Online dating and social media platforms can be useful tools for meeting new people. However, it's important to approach these platforms with caution and discernment. Be mindful of red flags and prioritize safety when communicating with strangers online. Use these platforms as a means to connect with people who share your interests and values. Be patient in your search for genuine connections.

Red flags are warning signs that indicate potential problems in a relationship. Pay attention to red flags such as controlling behavior, jealousy, gaslighting, and disrespect. If you see these signs, trust your instincts and prioritize your health. Don't ignore red flags in the hope that the person will change. Instead, protect yourself by setting boundaries and, if necessary, ending the relationship.

By cultivating self-love, a positive mindset, and proactive social engagement, you can attract positive people into your life. Remember to be patient, authentic, and open to new connections. By focusing on building genuine relationships based on mutual respect and understanding, you can create a fulfilling and supportive social circle.

18

Chapter 8

Setting Intentions and Goals

Defining Your Vision

The path to a new life starts with a clear picture of where you want to go. This vision is more than simply a dream; it is a strong intention that directs your activities and decisions. It is the compass that guides you through life's storms while keeping you focused on your goal.

To define your vision, first determine your passions and values. What excites you? What is most important to you in life? These answers will help you get to the heart of who you are and what you want to accomplish. Once you have established a thorough grasp of your passions and values, you may start to envision your ideal future.

Imagine yourself having the life you have always wanted. What does it look like? How are you feeling? What are you doing now? The more vivid and detailed your vision, the more impactful it will be. Allow yourself to be inspired and motivated by imagining your ideal future.

Setting SMART goals.

Once you have established a clear vision of your ideal future, it is time to turn it into concrete measures. This is where SMART goals come in. SMART goals are specific, measurable, achievable, relevant, and time-bound.

- **Specific:** Clearly state what you aim to accomplish. Instead of saying, "I want to be healthier," try saying, "I want to lose 10 pounds and exercise three times per week."
- **Measurable:** Create particular measures to track your progress. For example, you may chart your weight loss in pounds or inches, as well as the number of times you exercise per week.
- **Achievable:** Set goals that are tough but achievable. Avoid setting overly ambitious goals and ensure they correspond with your overarching vision and principles.
- **Time-bound:** Make explicit timelines for your goals. This will help you maintain your focus and motivation.

Breaking down enormous goals into smaller, more attainable steps can help them appear less daunting. For example, if you want to write a book, you may divide the process into smaller parts such as researching your topic, outlining your chapters, creating a draft, and editing your work.

Setting SMART objectives and breaking them down into smaller steps allows you to make considerable progress toward your vision.

Visualizing Your Future.

The Power of Visualization

Visualization is a powerful strategy for manifesting your wishes. You can program your subconscious mind to work toward your goals by visualizing them.

To imagine successfully, select a peaceful spot where you will not be inter-rupted. Close your eyes and take a few deep breaths to calm your mind and body. 1 Then, visualize yourself attaining your goals. Imagine yourself living the life of your dreams. Feel the emotions that come with success, such as joy, enthusiasm, and satisfaction.

The more frequently you imagine your goals, the more likely you are to accomplish them. Make it a regular habit to spend a few minutes envisioning your future.

Practicing gratitude.

Gratitude is a strong tool that can help you alter your perspective from scarcity to abundance. When you concentrate on the things you are grateful for, you open yourself up to receiving additional benefits.

To begin practicing thankfulness, begin by listing what you are grateful for. This could range from your health and family to your employment and home. Count your blessings and express gratitude daily.

You can also express thankfulness by keeping a gratitude notebook. Every day, write down three things for which you are grateful. Your perspective will gradually transform from one of scarcity to one of abundance.

By combining visualization and thankfulness, you can develop a powerful mentality that will assist you in realizing your dreams.

Action Steps

Overcoming Procrastination.

Procrastination is a common impediment to achieving our goals. Fear of failure, perfectionism, or a lack of desire are common causes.

To overcome procrastination, it is necessary to discover the root causes. Are you terrified of failing? Do you feel overwhelmed by the tasks at hand? You can address your procrastination once you know its cause.

One successful method for managing procrastination is to divide enormous activities into smaller, more manageable chunks. This can make the process less intimidating and help you stay focused. Another useful strategy is the Pomodoro strategy, which is working in focused 25-minute intervals separated by a 5-minute rest.

Creating effective time management strategies

Effective time management is critical to attaining your goals. You may make the best use of your time by prioritizing work and employing time management practices.

A time-tracking tool can help you manage your time more effectively. This might help you detect time-wasting activities and adapt your schedule. Another useful strategy is to use the Eisenhower Matrix, which allows you to prioritize tasks according to their urgency and importance.

Creating a Daily Routine

Creating a regular regimen might help you stay organized and productive. Setting a consistent plan will guarantee that you have time for work, rest, and recreation.

When planning your daily routine, make sure to schedule time for both focused work and leisure. It is also crucial to be adaptable and change your schedule as needed.

You can attain your aspirations and goals by overcoming procrastination, using effective time management skills, and establishing a daily routine.

Overcome Obstacles

Developing a growth mindset

A growth mindset is the concept that you can improve your abilities and intelligence through devotion and hard work. By adopting a growth mindset, you can see problems as chances to learn and improve.

To develop a development mindset, begin by reframing your thinking. Instead of thinking, "I am not good at this," say, "I can improve with practice." Accept obstacles as chances for learning and growth.

Learning From Failure

Failure is a normal part of life. Instead of perceiving failure as a setback, consider it a tremendous learning opportunity. Analyzing your blunders allows you to identify areas for growth and create new methods.

Remember that the goal is not to escape failure but to learn from it and go forward.

Seeking Support Having a strong support network can assist in overcoming difficulties and achieving goals. Surround yourself with positive, supportive others who believe in you.

Consider participating in a support group or hiring a coach or mentor. These people can offer counsel, encouragement, and accountability.

Celebrating Milestones

Recognizing and acknowledging achievements

Celebrating your accomplishments, no matter how minor, is critical for staying motivated and increasing self-esteem. When you take the time to appreciate your progress, you reinforce your confidence in your talents and motivate yourself to keep working toward your goals.

Whether you are finishing difficult work, attaining a fitness milestone, or simply getting through the day, take time to acknowledge your efforts. This could include rewarding yourself with something you appreciate, such as a favorite meal, a relaxing bath, or a hobby.

Practice Self-Compassion

Self-compassion entails treating oneself with care, understanding, and acceptance. Kindness to yourself helps you stay motivated and resilient in difficult times.

Avoid self-criticism and perfectionism. Instead, focus on progress rather than perfection. Remember that it is okay to make mistakes. Learn from them and move forward.

You may stay motivated, boost your self-esteem, and lead a full life by recognizing your accomplishments and practicing self-compassion.

Embracing change

Adapting to new situations.

Change is a necessary element of life. You can easily negotiate life's twists and turns if you work on your flexibility and adaptability.

When faced with a new circumstance, have an open mind. Be willing to attempt new things and get out of your comfort zone. Accept uncertainty as a chance for development and learning.

Let go of the past and embrace the future.

Holding onto the past can limit your ability to move forward. To embrace the future, let go of the past. This means learning from the past and moving forward.

Practice forgiveness, both toward yourself and others. Let go of bitterness and anger, and concentrate on the present.

Developing a Positive Outlook

A cheerful attitude can significantly improve your life. By being optimistic and grateful, you can attract positive experiences and possibilities.

Begin your day with a positive affirmation. Let go of negative thoughts and focus on the positive aspects of your life. A positive mindset can help you live a better and more rewarding life.

19

Chapter 9

Prioritizing Self-Care

Self-care is not a luxury; it is essential, particularly throughout the recovery process following narcissistic abuse. Taking care of your mind, body, and spirit restores overall health.

The value of self-care in recovery

When you have experienced the emotional anguish of narcissistic abuse, your self-esteem might suffer greatly. Self-care helps heal shattered self-esteem by prioritizing your needs and instilling a sense of value. It is a strong instrument that can help you regain your life and rediscover your true identity.

Identifying Your Self-Care Needs.

To properly practice self-care, you must first recognize your individual needs. Spend some time reflecting on what nurtures your soul. Do you yearn for physical activities, artistic outlets, or simply calm moments of solitude? Understanding your unique needs allows you to adjust your self-care practices to your specific tastes.

Developing a Self-Care Routine

Consistency is essential in self-care. Developing a consistent routine can help you prioritize your health and make it a non-negotiable aspect of your everyday life. Begin by allocating particular time blocks for things that invigorate you. Include these practices in your daily routine, whether it be a morning yoga session, an evening bath, or a leisurely walk in nature.

Practicing mindfulness and meditation

Mindfulness and meditation are effective methods of soothing the mind and reducing stress. By focusing on the present moment, you can let go of unpleasant thoughts and build a sense of calm. Begin with basic mindfulness activities like deep breathing and body scanning. As you advance, you can try guided meditations and mindfulness apps to help you improve your practice.

Engaging in physical activity.

Physical activity is important to both your physical and mental well-being. Endorphins, natural mood boosters, are released during exercise and can help with anxiety and despair. Find activities you enjoy, such as dancing, swimming, or hiking. Remember, the idea is to move your body while having fun.

Nourishing Your Body

Your physical health is inextricably tied to your psychological well-being. You may increase your energy levels, improve your mood, and improve your overall cognitive performance by feeding your body nutritious foods.

The Link Between Physical Health and Mental Well-being

The human body is a complicated system in which the health of one part can impact the overall health. Neglecting your bodily requirements might be detrimental to your mental health. In contrast, prioritizing your physical health can result in major gains in your mood, energy levels, and overall well-being.

Eating a balanced diet

A balanced diet gives your body the nutrition it requires to function properly. Incorporate a mix of fruits, vegetables, whole grains, lean meats, and healthy fats into your diet. Limit your consumption of processed meals, sugary beverages, and excessive levels of salt. You can improve your mental and emotional wellness by feeding your body nourishing foods.

Staying hydrated

Water is necessary for survival, and being hydrated is critical for overall health. Dehydration can cause weariness, headaches, and difficulties concentrating. Drink plenty of water throughout the day, especially if you are exercising or it is hot outside. You can also include hydrating items like fruits and vegetables in your diet.

Avoiding Harmful Substances.

Substance misuse can have a very negative influence on your physical and mental health. Alcohol, narcotics, and excessive coffee can alter your sleep patterns, cause anxiety, and lead to addiction. If you are struggling with substance misuse, seek expert treatment to address these issues.

Seeking professional nutritional guidance

If you have unique nutritional needs or concerns, speak with a licensed dietician. They can give you specialized advice on how to optimize your diet for your specific health goals. A nutritionist can assist you in developing a meal plan that fits your nutritional needs while also promoting your overall health.

Getting enough sleep.

Sleep is a critical component of human health that is frequently disregarded in our fast-paced environment. Adequate sleep is required for both physical and mental recovery, cognitive performance, and emotional stability.

The importance of sleep in recovery.

When healing from narcissistic abuse, your body and mind require plenty of time to heal. Sleep gives your body the rest and rejuvenation it needs to restore itself while also allowing your mind to process emotions and build new neural connections. Prioritizing sleep is essential for your overall health.

Establishing a Sleep Schedule

Creating a consistent sleep routine can help you sleep better. Every day, even on weekends, sleep and wake up at the same time. This helps to balance your body's internal schedule, resulting in more peaceful sleep.

Developing a Relaxing Bedtime Routine

A peaceful sleep routine helps alert your body that it is time to unwind. Create a relaxing regimen that includes activities such as reading, having a warm bath, and doing mild yoga. Avoid stimulating activities like watching TV or using electronic devices before bed, as the blue light emitted by these screens might disrupt your sleep.

Addressing Sleep Disorders

If you have chronic sleep difficulties like insomnia or sleep apnea, you should seek expert help. A sleep specialist can identify and treat underlying sleep issues, allowing you to get a better night's sleep.

Practice Sleep Hygiene.

Good sleep hygiene entails creating a sleep-friendly environment. Keep the bedroom dark, quiet, and chilly. Purchase a comfy mattress and pillows that support your body. Limit caffeine and alcohol consumption, particularly in the evening. By following these suggestions, you can improve your sleep environment and quality.

stress management.

Stress is a normal human experience, but prolonged stress can be harmful to your physical and mental health. Developing appropriate stress management strategies is critical for your overall well-being, especially when recovering from narcissistic abuse.

Recognizing Stress Triggers

The first stage in stress management is to identify your specific stress triggers. These can be work deadlines, money concerns, marital problems, or even specific persons or events. Once you have identified your triggers, you can devise measures to mitigate their influence.

Developing healthy coping mechanisms.

Healthy coping techniques can help you positively manage stress. Some effective tactics are:

1. **Physical Activity:** Exercise is an excellent stress reducer. Regular physical activity helps lower stress hormones and enhance your mood.
2. **Mindfulness and meditation:** These techniques can help you stay present and lessen worry.
3. **Time Management:** Good time management can help you feel more in control and less stressed.
4. **Social Support:** Connecting with loved ones and seeking help from friends and family can bring comfort and perspective.
5. **Creative Activities:** Painting, writing, or playing music can be therapeutic ways to express feelings and relieve stress.

Time Management Techniques

Effective time management can help you prioritize activities, decrease overwhelm, and increase overall productivity. Here are a few tips:

1. **Set realistic goals.** Break down enormous projects into smaller, more doable steps.
2. **Prioritize tasks.** Prioritize your tasks.
3. **Time Blocking:** Designate appropriate time blocks for different tasks.
4. **Avoid multitasking:** Focus on one task at a time to maximize efficiency.
5. Take short pauses to stay focused and rejuvenated.

Stress Reduction Techniques

In addition to the measures outlined above, you can utilize various other techniques to relieve stress:

1. Slow, deep breaths might help relax your nervous system.

2. Progressive Muscle Relaxation: Tensing and releasing various muscle groups can assist in relieving physical strain.

3. Aromatherapy: Essential oils such as lavender and chamomile can have a soothing effect.

4. Music can elicit positive emotions and relieve tension.

5. Spending time in nature might help you relax and reduce stress.

6. Seeking professional help is needed.

If you are having trouble managing stress on your own, you might consider seeking professional help. A therapist can offer advice and support as you establish appropriate coping techniques and deal with underlying difficulties.

Seeking Professional Help

While self-care and personal tactics are beneficial, professional assistance may be required to effectively heal from narcissistic abuse. A therapist can provide a safe and supportive environment in which to process your experiences, develop coping strategies, and move toward healing.

When to Seek Therapy?

Consider therapy if you experience the following:

1. Sustained feelings of melancholy, anxiety, or hopelessness

2. Having difficulty trusting others.

3. Difficulty developing healthy connections

4. Self-destructive behavior.

5. Suicidal ideation or acts.

Choosing a therapist

When choosing a therapist, look for someone who has expertise with trauma and abuse. Consider characteristics such as their credentials, therapeutic approach, and personality. It is critical to feel comfortable and safe with your therapist; therefore, do not be afraid to interview candidates before making a decision.

The Therapeutic Process

Individual therapy, group therapy, and couples therapy are all options for treatment. The approach you use will be determined by your demands and goals. During therapy, you may discuss your prior experiences, devise coping methods, and strive to recover your self-esteem.

Medication Management

In some situations, medication may be used to treat symptoms of anxiety, depression, or other mental health issues. A psychiatrist can evaluate your situation and provide suitable medicine. It is critical to collaborate closely with your psychiatrist to monitor your medication and modify the amount as needed.

The importance of ongoing support.

Recovery from narcissistic abuse is a journey rather than a destination. Even after you have completed therapy, you should continue to prioritize your mental health and seek continuing assistance. This could include going to support groups, practicing self-care, and maintaining positive relationships.

One step at a time is fine when healing. You may overcome the obstacles of narcissistic abuse and live a successful life by focusing on self-care, obtaining professional treatment when necessary, and exercising patience and compassion

20

Chapter 10

Embracing the Journey

The road to rehabilitation is long, not short. It is a voyage full of twists and turns, highs and lows. Remember, you are not alone on this journey. Many people have walked this path before you, and many more will follow.

Reflecting on your past experiences is an effective strategy for personal growth. Consider the obstacles you have overcome, the strength you have developed, and the lessons you have learned. Acknowledging your development allows you to build on your accomplishments and attack future challenges with fresh confidence.

It is critical to appreciate your accomplishments, no matter how minor they may appear. Whether it is a day without a panic attack, a successful interaction with a tough individual, or simply getting out of bed in the morning, every achievement is a step forward. Celebrate your accomplishments, big and small, and reward yourself for your hard work.

Remember to practice self-compassion as you continue on your journey. Be kind to yourself, and do not beat yourself up over losses or mistakes. Everyone has problems, and how we respond to them is what matters most. Practice self-care, prioritize your health, and surround yourself with positive people that bring you up.

By embracing the journey and appreciating your accomplishments, you may go forward with hope and optimism. Remember that the destination is worth the trip.

The Power of Hope

Hope is a powerful force that can help us get through the darkest of circumstances. It is a conviction that better days are ahead and that things will eventually get better. When we foster hope, we allow ourselves to heal, grow, and find pleasure.

To create hope, focus on the positive parts of your life. Recognize your strengths, successes, and those who love and support you. You can counteract negative thoughts and emotions by focusing on the positive.

Remember that hope is not wishful thinking. It is the belief that you can overcome obstacles and build a brighter future for yourself. To foster this belief, set realistic goals and make tiny efforts toward reaching them. Each step, no matter how tiny, puts you closer to your goal.

Let go of fear and doubt as you work toward recovery. These negative feelings can hold you back from realizing your full potential. Instead, embrace courage and believe in your ability to conquer problems.

Remember the Bible's words: "For I know the plans I have for you," declares the Lord, "plans to prosper you and not to harm you, plans to give you hope and a future" (Jeremiah 29:11). Trust in God's plan for your life and have faith that He will guide you through every obstacle.

You can achieve your full potential and a brighter future by nurturing hope, letting go of fear, and trusting in God's plan.

Continued Growth and Evolution.

As you begin your healing and recovery path, keep in mind that personal growth is an ongoing process. It is not a goal, but rather an ongoing journey of self-discovery and progress.

Lifelong learning is one of the most effective strategies to grow and evolve. Look for ways to broaden your knowledge and abilities, whether through books, classes, or seminars. Learning new things allows you to push yourself, excite your brain, and obtain fresh insights.

Do not be scared to venture outside of your comfort zone and take on new challenges. Taking risks and trying new things allows you to find hidden talents and strengths. Remember that true growth occurs when we overcome problems.

Being adaptive and open to change is essential as you navigate life's ups and downs. Accept change as a chance for development and transformation. Being adaptable and open-minded allows you to adjust to new situations and embrace new chances.

According to Romans 12:2, we should be "renewing our minds." By refreshing our brains, we can overcome negative thought patterns and embrace a more positive attitude toward life.

By committing to lifelong learning, accepting difficulties, and renewing our brains, we can continue to grow and evolve into the finest versions of ourselves.

Sharing your story

One of the most effective ways to heal and grow is to share your story. Sharing your experiences with others can make them feel less alone and inspire them to embark on their healing journey.

Joining support groups and online forums might help you connect with people who understand what you are going through. Sharing your experiences and listening to others' tales can bring comfort, support, and a sense of belonging.

Sharing your story might also serve as a source of inspiration and hope for others. Your remarks can encourage people to seek assistance, leave harmful situations, and create a brighter future.

Remember the Bible's words: "Therefore encourage one another and build each other up, just as you are doing." (1 Thessalonians 5:11). By encouraging and strengthening others, we can generate a positive and hopeful ripple effect.

Sharing your story allows you to not only benefit yourself but also positively touch the lives of others.

Living your best life.

As you continue on your path of healing and growth, remember to emphasize your pleasure and satisfaction. This entails creating a life that provides you with joy, purpose, and fulfillment.

Pursuing your hobbies and aspirations is essential for living your greatest life. Pursuing your passion, whether it is a hobby, a career, or a creative pursuit, may bring you a lot of happiness and contentment. Do not let fear or self-doubt keep you back. Take the chance and follow your heart.

Building meaningful relationships is another critical component of a successful life. Surround yourself with good, supportive people who will encourage and inspire you. Maintain your relationships with family, friends, and loved ones, and be willing to make new connections.

Remember to exercise self-care and put your well-being first. Make time for yourself to unwind, recharge, and do what you enjoy. Self-care, whether it involves reading a book, going on a walk, or simply spending time in nature, is critical for preserving your mental and emotional wellness.

As you endeavor to live your best life, believe in God's purpose for you. He knows what is best for you, and He has a wonderful future planned. Trust in His timing and have trust that everything will turn out as it should.

You can live a satisfying and meaningful life by pursuing your passions, cultivating meaningful connections, practicing self-care, and believing in God's plan.

21

Building A New Life

Recognizing the Patterns of Abuse

The insidious nature of narcissistic abuse frequently makes it difficult to detect, as it is concealed behind a veneer of charm and deception. Narcissists excel at portraying themselves as perfect while slowly weakening their victims' self-esteem. This can result in a years-long cycle of abuse, leaving victims bewildered, alienated, and emotionally depleted.

One of the most typical narcissistic methods is gaslighting. This entails convincing a victim to mistrust their views of reality. For example, a narcissist may deny saying something cruel even if the victim fully recalls the episode. A victim may question their sanity and become more dependent on the narcissist for validation.

Another typical method is triangulation, which entails bringing in a third party to add drama and confusion. This might be as easy as disclosing personal information about the victim to a friend or family member or as complicated as starting a love triangle. The idea is to keep the victim off balance and rely on the narcissist for emotional support.

Narcissists also frequently utilize projection. This entails assigning unde-sirable characteristics to the victim. For example, an insecure narcissist may accuse their partner of jealousy or control. This can be an effective manipulation strategy since it causes the victim to question their motivations and conduct.

Silent treatment is another form of emotional abuse that narcissists frequently employ. This includes withholding affection and communication as a form of punishment. The purpose is to make the victim feel guilty and frightened, forcing them to apologize for something they did not commit.

Love bombing is another method used by narcissists to seduce their victims. This includes showering the victim with compassion, attention, and gifts. However, this is frequently a fleeting phase, as the narcissist gradually withdraws their devotion and begins to devalue the victim.

It is critical to detect these abusive behaviors and understand how they might affect your mental and emotional well-being. Recognizing the indicators of narcissistic abuse allows you to protect yourself and break the cycle.

Understanding Manipulation Tactics

Gaslighting, a particularly subtle form of manipulation, is typical of nar-cissistic abuse. Narcissists skillfully distort reality, forcing their victims to question their senses. They may deny saying or doing something, despite incontrovertible evidence to the contrary. Victims may become confused, disoriented, and question their sanity as a result. Gaslighting can gradually destroy a person's self-esteem and feelings of value.

Triangulation is another popular method employed by narcissists to foment dissension and preserve power. By involving a third party, they can induce drama, envy, and misunderstanding. For example, a narcissist may disclose intimate information about their relationship to a friend or family member, or they may flirt with others to make their partner feel insecure. This can lead to feelings of isolation and mistrust since the victim is always questioning their perceptions and relationships.

Projection is a protective strategy that narcissists frequently utilize to avoid accepting responsibility for their acts. They may accuse their victims of the same actions they engage in. For example, a narcissistic parent may accuse their child of being greedy or manipulative, when in actuality, the parent is displaying similar traits. This can be a strong manipulation strategy since it causes the victim to question their judgment and feel awful about the narcissist's behavior.

The silent treatment is a type of emotional abuse that narcissists frequently employ to punish and control their victims. By withholding affection, attention, and communication, they can cause their victims to feel uneasy, insecure, and needy for their approval. This can be especially detrimental in relationships since it can make the sufferer feel lonely and alone.

Love bombing is another method used by narcissists to seduce their victims. They may show their victims affection, attention, and presence, making them feel unique and loved. However, this is frequently a fleeting phase, as the narcissist gradually withdraws their affection and begins to devalue their victim. This might make the sufferer feel confused, wounded, and mistrustful of their judgment.

Victims of narcissistic abuse can begin to discern patterns of conduct and protect themselves from future harm if they know these manipulation strategies.

Setting boundaries and limits.

Setting and enforcing boundaries is one of the most important steps toward breaking free from the cycle of narcissistic abuse. Boundaries are invisible lines that define what constitutes acceptable and inappropriate behavior. Setting firm boundaries will preserve your emotional and psychological well-being and keep the narcissist from manipulating and controlling you.

Communicate Your Needs

The first step in defining limits is to properly define your requirements and expectations. This can be difficult, especially if you are accustomed to pleasing others or avoiding confrontation. However, it is critical to be assertive and direct. Let the narcissist know what behavior is undesirable and what repercussions await them if they continue to violate your limits.

Saying No.

Learning to say no is another essential ability for creating limits. It is acceptable to deny requests, even if it means disappointing someone. Remember, you do not have to please everyone. Saying no prioritizes your own needs and well-being.

Setting limits on contact

If you are in a relationship with a narcissist, you may need to limit contact. This might be challenging, particularly if you have children or share property. However, it is critical to safeguard yourself against further abuse. You might want to try going no-contact, which involves ending all communication with the narcissist.

Enforcing boundaries.

Once you have established boundaries, it is critical to enforce them consistently. This entails adhering to your boundaries, even when the narcissist tries to push them. It may be important to isolate yourself from the narcissist or even terminate the connection entirely.

Remember that setting limits is not selfish. It is an act of self-care. Protecting your emotional and psychological well-being empowers you to live a happier and healthier life.

Breaking ties and going without contact

Cutting ties and avoiding contact with a narcissist is frequently a critical step toward healing and rehabilitation. While it may appear frightening, making this decision has the potential to greatly improve your mental and emotional well-being.

The Importance of No Contact

No contact is a tactic that entails cutting off all communication with the narcissist. This includes telephone conversations, messages, emails, and social media. It may also entail avoiding places where you know you may encounter them. While it may appear severe, no contact is frequently the only option to escape the cycle of abuse.

When you have contact with a narcissist, you are continually subjected to their manipulation and gaslighting. This can make it tough to recover and move forward. Going with no contact means distancing yourself from the toxic atmosphere and allowing yourself space and time to recover.

Creating a No-Contact Plan

To successfully implement a no-contact plan, a specific strategy must be developed. This may include barring the narcissist's phone number, deleting their contact information, and unfollowing them on social media. You could also consider changing your phone number or email address.

It is also critical to advise shared friends and family members of your intention to maintain no contact. This will assist in reducing any unintentional interaction and prevent the narcissist from exploiting others to approach you.

Dealing with Breakup Anxiety.

Breaking up with a narcissist can be a difficult event. You may feel grief, loss, and anxiety. It is critical to accept these emotions and allow yourself to grieve the end of the relationship.

Practicing self-care can help you cope with breakup anxiety. This could include spending time with loved ones, engaging in hobbies, or seeking expert aid. Avoiding triggers like songs or places that remind you of the narcissist is also important.

Resisting Temptation

One of the most difficult aspects of maintaining no contact is fighting the urge to contact the narcissist. This might be especially challenging during times of stress or loneliness. Realize that any contact with the narcissist, no matter how brief, may slow your healing.

To resist temptation, focus on your goals and the reasons you chose no contact. It may also be beneficial to remind yourself of the narcissist's detrimental influence on your life.

Cutting ties and going without contact is a crucial step toward reclaiming control and rebuilding your life.

Embracing your fear of the unknown

Breaking free from a narcissistic relationship can be a difficult process fraught with anxiety and dread of the unknown. However, it is critical to embrace these feelings and make the transition to a healthier and happier future.

Confronting Fear

The first step toward overcoming fear is to acknowledge its existence. Denying or concealing fear simply exacerbates it. Instead, accept your fears and allow yourself to experience them. Acknowledging your worries allows you to begin to understand their underlying causes and build techniques to control them.

Developing Self-Confidence

Developing self-confidence is critical for overcoming anxiety and uncertainty. Remind yourself of your abilities, achievements, and resilience. Celebrate your accomplishments, no matter how minor they may appear. Surround yourself with positive individuals who believe in you.

Take Small Steps

Breaking down major goals into smaller, more attainable tasks might help reduce feelings of overwhelm. Concentrate on one activity at a time and enjoy every modest accomplishment. This progressive approach can help you gain momentum and stay motivated.

Seeking Support Do not hesitate to seek help from friends, family, or a therapist. Talking to someone you trust can bring you comfort, perspective, and useful counsel. A therapist can provide expert advice and techniques to help you deal with the emotional issues of leaving a narcissistic relationship.

Remember: you are not alone. Many people have successfully recovered from narcissistic abuse and rebuilt their lives. You, too, can accomplish this with courage, determination, and support.

22

Chapter 2

Challenging Negative Self-Beliefs

The first step toward reclaiming your self-worth is to recognize and question any negative self-beliefs that have become embedded in your mind. Narcissistic abuse frequently entails a concerted effort to undermine your self-esteem, leaving you feeling worthless, incompetent, and unable. It is critical to identify these incorrect ideas and replace them with positive affirmations.

Becoming aware of your inner critic is a useful strategy for spotting self-sabotaging thoughts. This inner voice, which is frequently harsh and judgmental, can consistently weaken your self-esteem. Pay attention to any negative ideas that occur, especially those that center on your perceived flaws or limitations.

Once you have discovered the negative beliefs, it is time to question their validity. Are these thoughts true reflections of yourself, or are they distorted perceptions caused by the narcissist's manipulation? Remember that the narcissist's purpose is to manipulate you by making you question yourself. By challenging the truth of these negative thoughts, you can begin to break free from their hold.

Positive affirmations can help you overcome negative self-talk. These are strong comments that can change your attitude and increase your self-esteem. For example, instead of thinking, "I am not good enough," say, "I am worthy of love and respect," or "I am capable and strong."

The more positive affirmations you use, the more firmly they become engraved in your subconscious mind. As a result, you will gain confidence in yourself and your talents.

Cognitive behavioral therapy (CBT) is another effective method for confronting negative self-beliefs. CBT is a type of treatment that enables you to recognize and confront problematic thought patterns. Learning to notice and reframe negative ideas can dramatically enhance your mental and emotional health.

A CBT therapist can help you identify negative thoughts, assess their correctness, and replace them with more positive and realistic ones. Regular practice can help you build a more positive and empowering mindset.

Journaling is an effective strategy for recognizing and overcoming negative self-beliefs. Writing down your thoughts and feelings might help you gain a better understanding of your internal world. You may find previously unknown tendencies of negative thinking.

Journaling can also help you monitor your progress in addressing negative self-beliefs. As you replace negative ideas with positive affirmations, you can chronicle and celebrate your accomplishments. This positive reinforcement will increase your self-esteem.

Remember that addressing negative self-beliefs is a continuous process. It takes time and care to rewire your thinking processes. Be gentle with yourself and recognize your accomplishments, no matter how tiny. With constant effort and practice, you may overcome your negative self-talk and adopt a more positive and empowering perspective.

Practice Self-Compassion.

Self-compassion is an essential component of self-recovery. It entails treating yourself with care, empathy, and acceptance, much like you would a close friend. Self-compassion can help you heal from the wounds of narcissistic abuse and gain a better sense of self-worth.

Self-kindness is a basic component of self-compassion. Instead of berating yourself for your mistakes or weaknesses, show yourself compassion and empathy. Remind yourself that everyone makes errors and that it is acceptable to be flawed.

When you make a mistake, do not criticize yourself. Instead, concentrate on learning from the situation and moving forward. Remember that making mistakes is a normal part of the human experience. Being compassionate to yourself can help you break the cycle of self-blame and shame.

Accepting your flaws is another essential component of self-compassion. Nobody is flawless, and it is ridiculous to expect yourself to be. Accept your defects and oddities, and understand that they are part of what makes you special.

Instead of striving for perfection, prioritize development. Celebrate your accomplishments, no matter how minor they may appear. Accepting your flaws allows you to live a more honest life and relieves the pressure to be flawless.

Practicing self-compassion requires letting go of self-criticism. Self-criticism can be a severe and relentless inner critic, continuously undermining your self-esteem. You can break out of this negative loop by noticing and questioning your critical ideas.

When self-critical thoughts come, pause and breathe. Consider whether you would use such harsh and judgmental language with a friend. The most likely response is no. Treat yourself with the same respect and compassion you would show a loved one.

Self-kindness, embracing faults, and letting go of self-criticism might help you create a greater feeling of self-compassion. This will allow you to recover from the wounds of narcissistic abuse and develop a stronger, more resilient sense of self.

Remember that self-compassion is a skill that requires time and practice to acquire. Be patient with yourself and recognize your accomplishments, no matter how tiny. With constant work, you can learn to be kind and empathetic to yourself.

Learn to Love Yourself

Learning to love oneself is an important step in self-recovery. It requires building a strong sense of self-worth and acceptance. When you love yourself, you can establish healthy boundaries, attract wonderful relationships, and lead a satisfying life.

Prioritizing self-care is an essential component of self-love. This entails taking time for yourself to unwind, refuel, and engage in activities that offer you delight. Make time for soul-nourishing activities, such as having a long bath, reading a book, or spending time in nature.

Prioritizing self-care may also entail establishing boundaries with others. It is critical to set appropriate limits to protect your mental and physical well-being. This could include declining requests that do not correspond with your values or priorities or spending less time with toxic people.

Another important component of self-love is creating realistic goals for oneself. It is critical to set attainable goals and avoid striving for perfection. Remember: progress, not perfection, is the key to success.

When you set reasonable expectations, you are less likely to be disappointed or frustrated. Instead, you can concentrate on making consistent progress toward your goals.

Celebrating your accomplishments, no matter how minor, is a crucial element of self-love. Take the time to recognize your achievements and thank yourself for your hard work. This positive feedback can increase your self-esteem and drive you to keep working toward your goals.

Prioritizing self-care, setting reasonable objectives, and appreciating your accomplishments can help you develop a strong sense of self-love. This will help you live a more fulfilling and true life.

"Developing Self-Confidence"

Building self-confidence is critical to recovering your power and living a successful life. When you believe in yourself, you are more inclined to take risks, follow your dreams, and overcome obstacles.

Stepping outside of your comfort zone is an effective approach to enhance your self-confidence. By pushing yourself to do new things, you can broaden your strengths and learn new skills. This could be taking a class, volunteering on a new project, or simply trying out a new interest.

Remember that it is normal to feel uncomfortable or anxious when you move outside of your comfort zone. Accept these sentiments as possibilities for progress. With each difficulty you overcome, your self-confidence grows stronger.

Taking chances is another essential component of developing self-confidence. While it is necessary to use caution, do not let fear prevent you from achieving your objectives. Taking prudent risks can lead to new possibilities and experiences.

Remember that failure is a normal part of the learning process. Do not let setbacks depress you. Instead, see these as opportunities to learn and grow. You can cultivate a resilient mindset by accepting failure as a necessary step toward achievement.

Mastering new talents is another effective approach to enhancing self-esteem. Whether it is learning a new language, playing a musical instrument, or mastering a new software program, obtaining new talents can boost your confidence and capability.

As you learn and progress, appreciate your accomplishments, no matter how minor they may appear. This positive reinforcement will keep you motivated and moving forward.

Visualizing achievement is another powerful approach to increasing self-esteem. Imagine yourself attaining your goals to develop a positive mental image that will motivate and inspire you.

Spend some time each day visualizing yourself succeeding. Imagine yourself conquering obstacles, attaining your goals, and enjoying the life you want. The more you picture success, the more likely you are to attain it.

Stepping outside of your comfort zone, taking risks, learning new abilities, and picturing achievement can help you establish a solid foundation of self-confidence. This will help you live a more fulfilling and true life.

Accepting Your Authentic Self

Embracing your real self is a process of self-discovery and acceptance. It entails discovering your own identity, expressing yourself authentically, and living a life that is consistent with your ideals.

Take some time to reflect on who you truly are. This could be journaling, meditation, or simply being alone with your thoughts. Ask yourself questions such as, "What are my passions?" What are my values? "What brings me true happiness?"

As you explore your inner world, you may come upon hidden talents, interests, and ambitions. Do not be frightened to accept these new facets of yourself. They may help you live a more fulfilling and meaningful life.

Being honest and transparent with others is essential when expressing your real self. This involves expressing your views, feelings, and opinions, even if they are not always popular. It also includes establishing boundaries and saying no when required.

Showing your true self will attract people who value you. You will also develop stronger, more meaningful relationships.

Another key component of embracing your real self is letting go of the need to please others. People-pleasing entails constantly seeking approval from others, frequently at the expense of one's own needs and wants. By letting go of the need for validation, you can be yourself.

Remember, it is good to disappoint folks sometimes. Setting boundaries and prioritizing your own needs can allow you to live a more real and fulfilling life rather than try to please everyone else.

Living a values-driven life entails making decisions that reflect your most deeply held views and convictions. Making unpleasant decisions may be required, but the result will be worthwhile.

Living a genuine life, true to yourself, will provide you with a deeper feeling of purpose and significance. You will also be able to positively change the globe.

Embracing oneself is a journey that requires time and effort. Be patient with yourself and applaud your accomplishments. You can experience more freedom, joy, and contentment by discovering your actual identity, expressing yourself honestly, and living a life that is consistent with your principles.

23

Chapter 3

Processing Trauma and Grief

The aftermath of narcissistic abuse frequently leaves victims dealing with a complex mix of trauma and grief. Understanding the scope of this emotional anguish is critical before going on the path to recovery. The first step is to acknowledge the abuse's significant psychological consequences.

Narcissistic abuse, known for its insidious nature, can undermine a person's sense of self, leaving them feeling worthless, confused, and alone. Narcissists' gaslighting, manipulation, and emotional manipulation can distort reality, making it difficult for victims to tell the difference between truth and lies. This cognitive dissonance can cause a significant sensation of disorientation and perplexity.

As victims begin to grasp the toxic nature of the connection, a grieving process is generally initiated. They may lament the loss of the idealized spouse, the shattered dreams, and the damage done to their self-esteem. This grief can take many forms, including sadness, anger, guilt, and humiliation.

It is critical to recognize and validate these emotions. Suppressing or ignoring them can slow the healing process. Victims might begin to alleviate their emotional weight by expressing their feelings. Journaling, talking to trustworthy friends or family members, or getting professional therapy can all provide a safe environment for you to express your emotions without being judged.

Seeking professional help, such as therapy or counseling, can be quite beneficial in processing trauma and sorrow. Therapists educated in trauma-informed care can offer direction, support, and evidence-based strategies to assist individuals in processing their experiences. Cognitive-behavioral therapy (CBT) can be especially effective for addressing negative thought patterns and building healthy coping skills.

Self-care techniques, such as mindfulness and meditation, can also aid in the healing process. These activities can help people become more aware of their thoughts and emotions, enabling them to better handle stress and anxiety. Activities that encourage relaxation, such as yoga, deep breathing, or spending time in nature, can improve emotional well-being.

Joining support groups helps foster a sense of belonging and understanding. Connecting with individuals who have been through similar circumstances can provide comfort, validation, and practical guidance. Sharing stories and providing support can be an effective approach to healing together.

As victims traverse the intricacies of trauma and sorrow, it is critical to remember that healing is a process, not a destination. Progress may be slow, and setbacks may occur. However, by taking little steps, individuals can eventually reclaim their emotional well-being and emerge stronger from the experience.

Establishing Healthy Coping Mechanisms

Once the initial shock and anguish of narcissistic abuse have subsided, it is critical to build appropriate coping methods to deal with the emotional repercussions. These practices can help people manage the barriers of recovery and develop resilience.

One of the most important phases is to identify and replace any unhealthy coping mechanisms that may have formed as a result of the abuse. These could include substance misuse, an overreliance on dysfunctional relationships, or self-destructive behavior. Recognizing these habits is the first step in breaking free from them.

Positive coping methods provide healthier choices. Regular physical activity, such as exercise or sports, can increase endorphin levels, boost mood, and reduce stress. It can also improve self-esteem and energy levels.

Mindfulness and meditation can be effective stress-reduction techniques. These approaches include focusing on the present moment, embracing thoughts and feelings without judgment, and building an inner serenity. Regular practice can help reduce ruminating, improve emotional regulation, and boost general well-being.

Deep breathing exercises can quickly and effectively relax the nervous system. Slow, deep breathing can help people lower their pulse rate, reduce muscle tension, and relax. This approach is especially useful for treating anxiety and panic episodes.

Spending time in nature has been demonstrated to provide significant mental health advantages. Exposure to natural areas can reduce stress, improve mood, and boost vitality. Hiking, gardening, or simply spending time outside can help you connect with nature and achieve a sense of calm and tranquility.

Establishing a solid support network is critical for emotional well-being. Surrounding oneself with supportive friends, family members, or a therapist can give a secure environment in which to communicate feelings, receive encouragement, and gain perspective. These partnerships can provide a sense of belonging while reducing feelings of isolation.

By implementing these healthy coping methods into their daily lives, people can gradually restore their emotional resilience and nurture inner calm. It is critical to remember that healing is a process, and progress may not always be linear. Individuals who practice patience, self-compassion, and tenacity can emerge from the hardships of narcissistic abuse stronger and empowered.

Managing Anxiety and Depression.

The mental anguish caused by narcissistic abuse can frequently lead to the development of anxiety and despair. These mental health issues can have a substantial influence on someone's quality of life, making it difficult to function and enjoy it. It is critical to recognize the signs and symptoms of these illnesses and seek appropriate care.

Anxiety disorders are defined by excessive anxiety, fear, and nervousness. Common symptoms include restlessness, exhaustion, difficulty concentrating, irritability, muscle tightness, and sleep problems. In severe cases, panic episodes can occur, characterized by intense dread and physical symptoms such as high heart rate, perspiration, and shortness of breath.

In contrast, depression is a mood illness characterized by persistent feelings of sadness, helplessness, and worthlessness. Depression symptoms may include a loss of interest in activities, changes in eating and sleep patterns, exhaustion, problems focusing, and suicidal ideation.

If you are experiencing symptoms of anxiety or despair, you should get professional treatment. A mental health specialist can identify your illness and make suitable treatment recommendations. These can include treatment, medicine, or a mix of the two.

Cognitive-behavioral therapy (CBT) is a sort of treatment that can help with anxiety and depression. CBT enables people to identify and fight problematic thought patterns, as well as create healthy coping methods. You can modify your feelings by changing your way of thinking.

Medication can also be useful in treating anxiety and depression. Antidepressants and anti-anxiety drugs can help regulate mood and alleviate symptoms. It is critical to consult with a doctor to determine the appropriate prescription and dosage for you.

In addition to professional assistance, various self-help practices can be useful in controlling anxiety and depression. This includes:

1. **Using relaxation techniques:** Deep breathing, meditation, and yoga can all assist in quieting the mind and body.
2. **Regular physical activity:** exercise can help improve mood, reduce stress, and promote sleep.
3. **Getting adequate sleep:** aim for 7–8 hours of sleep each night.
4. **Eating a nutritious diet** can supply the nutrients your body requires to function properly.
5. **Limiting alcohol and drug consumption:** Alcohol and drugs can exacerbate feelings of anxiety and sadness.
6. **Creating a solid support system:** Spending time with loved ones can provide emotional support and alleviate feelings of isolation.

Remember to be patient with yourself. Healing takes time, and there may be obstacles in the process. You can manage anxiety and depression while also leading a full life by obtaining professional help, practicing self-care, and creating healthy coping skills.

Developing Emotional Resilience

Emotional resilience, sometimes known as "mental toughness," is the ability to recover from misfortune and maintain emotional equilibrium in the face of obstacles. Cultivating this resilience is critical for long-term well-being and can greatly improve your ability to deal with stress and adversity.

The development of emotional intelligence is an important component of emotional resilience. This includes understanding and managing your own emotions, as well as recognizing and responding to others' emotions. By becoming more aware of your emotional state, you can detect triggers, manage stress, and respond to circumstances in a more productive manner.

Learning to adapt to change is another critical component of emotional resilience. Life is full of unexpected twists and turns, and being able to adapt to new situations can help minimize stress and anxiety. By seeing change as an opportunity for growth and learning, you can cultivate a more adaptable attitude.

Building self-efficacy, or confidence in one's ability to succeed, is critical for emotional resilience. Setting attainable objectives, breaking down difficult activities into smaller ones, and celebrating your successes can all help enhance your self-esteem. Believing in oneself allows you to overcome obstacles and endure in the face of hardship.

Gratitude is an effective technique to develop a positive mentality and increase emotional resilience. By focusing on the positive things in your life, you can change your perspective and lessen unpleasant thoughts and sensations. Gratitude can also improve relationships by increasing feelings of connection and belonging.

To cultivate a positive mindset, challenge negative beliefs and replace them with positive affirmations. Positive self-talk and visualization of success can help you retrain your brain to think more favorably. Positive thinking can help you minimize stress, improve your mood, and feel better overall.

You may enhance your emotional resilience and lay a solid basis for long-term well-being by developing emotional intelligence, adapting to change, increasing self-efficacy, practicing gratitude, and creating a positive mentality. Remember that resilience is a skill that can be learned and improved over time.

Find Peace Within Yourself

Finding inner peace is a path that necessitates self-awareness, self-compassion, and the ability to let go of the past. It is the process of discovering and accepting your true self, free of the expectations and judgments of others.

Embracing isolation can be an effective technique for self-discovery and inner tranquility. Spending time alone allows you to connect with your thoughts and emotions without interruptions or other constraints. It promotes meditation, contemplation, and creative expression.

Self-compassion entails treating oneself with kindness, understanding, and forgiveness. Instead of berating yourself for mistakes or failings, practice self-compassion by admitting your flaws and accepting yourself for who you are.

Letting go of control is another important part of achieving inner peace. We typically try to control situations, people, and results, which can lead to dissatisfaction and disappointment. Accepting that we cannot control everything allows us to let go of the drive for control and achieve greater calm and acceptance.

Trusting in the process of life is vital for achieving inner peace. Often, we worry about the future or linger on the past, but this prevents us from truly appreciating the present. We can let go of our fears and accept uncertainty with faith that everything will work out as planned.

Finding inner peace is a personal process that involves patience, perseverance, and a willingness to explore one's inner world. A deep sense of calm and contentment can be achieved by embracing isolation, practicing self-compassion, letting go of control, and trusting the process.

24

Chapter 4

Rediscovering Your Passions

Finding your passions is the first step toward recovering your inner strength. These are the activities that enliven your spirit, bring you delight, and make you feel fully alive. Perhaps you once enjoyed painting, playing an instrument, or writing poetry. Perhaps you enjoyed gardening, hiking, or simply spending time outside. Whatever your passions are, now is the time to revive them.

Start by reflecting on your past. Consider which activities offered you the most joy and contentment. What were your favorite childhood activities? What hobbies did you have in your youth? What made you feel so passionate? As you dig through your recollections, you could be shocked to find forgotten interests and long-lost passions.

Be open to new hobbies and activities. Trying something new can help you find your hidden talents and hobbies. Consider taking a class, joining a club, or volunteering for a subject you are passionate about. These experiences will allow you to meet new people, gain new skills, and widen your perspectives.

Rekindling old passions can be as satisfying. If you used to enjoy painting, for example, why not take up a brush and get creative again? If you previously played a musical instrument, dust it off and practice. You may be surprised how quickly your abilities return after years of inactivity.

Prioritizing passion tasks is critical to reconnecting with your inner power. Make time for the things you enjoy, even if it means forgoing other pursuits. Set aside time each day or week to focus on your passion projects. This will help you maintain your focus and motivation.

Finding joy in creative activities can be an effective method to express yourself and connect with your inner creativity. Whether you prefer painting, writing, music, or dance, creative expression can bring you enormous joy and fulfillment. Never be scared to experiment and try new things. The more you practice, the more creative you will be.

Remember that rediscovering your hobbies is a journey rather than a destination. It may take time to rekindle old flames and find new ones. Be patient with yourself, and enjoy the process. As you reconnect with your passions, you will feel more energized, fulfilled, and connected to your authentic self.

Setting achievable goals

After you have rediscovered your hobbies, the following stage is to establish attainable goals. This will help you stay focused and motivated as you pursue your dreams. Breaking down large goals into smaller, more attainable steps makes them appear less daunting. For example, if you aim to write a novel, you could divide it into smaller parts, like developing a character outline, writing one chapter per week, or revising and proofreading your work.

Setting SMART goals is another excellent approach. The acronym SMART stands for Specific, Measurable, Achievable, Relevant, and Timebound. Setting concrete, quantifiable, and achievable goals will help you track your progress and stay on track. Instead of declaring, "I want to be a better writer," make a SMART goal such as, "I will write 1,000 words per day for the next month."

Creating a vision board can also help keep you motivated. A vision board is a visual depiction of your aims and aspirations. You can make a physical vision board by cutting out photos and quotes from magazines and newspapers or a digital vision board with a program like Canva. Visualizing your goals might help you stay inspired and focused.

Tracking your success is critical for maintaining motivation. Keep track of your daily, weekly, and monthly goals in a journal or planner. Celebrate your victories, no matter how minor they may appear. This will help you remain cheerful and motivated.

Celebrating milestones is a vital aspect of attaining your goals. When you hit an important milestone, take the time to celebrate your accomplishment. This could include buying yourself something special, spending time with loved ones, or simply taking a moment to unwind and rejuvenate.

Remember that creating realistic objectives is a journey, not a race. Do not be discouraged if you do not attain your goals right away. Simply keep taking little steps and celebrating your accomplishments along the way.

Creating a Support Network

Building a solid support network is critical on your path to self-recovery. Surrounding yourself with positive and supportive individuals can offer you the encouragement, understanding, and love you require to heal and grow.

Reaching out to loved ones is an excellent way to begin. Share your thoughts and feelings with trusted friends and family. Tell them how you are feeling and what you need from them. Honest and open conversation can build your relationships and provide much-needed emotional support.

Joining support groups can be beneficial. These groups offer a safe and supportive environment in which you can connect with others who have been through similar circumstances. Sharing your story and hearing the tales of others might make you feel less alone and more understood.

Connecting with online communities can also provide vital support. There are numerous online forums and social media groups dedicated to assisting victims of narcissistic abuse. People from all over the world may provide you with support, advice, and encouragement.

Seeking professional assistance is another crucial step toward developing a support network. A therapist or counselor can give you the resources and skills you need to heal and recover. They can assist you with overcoming your trauma, developing healthy coping skills, and improving your self-esteem.

Developing meaningful relationships is critical to long-term well-being. These partnerships can bring you love, support, and companionship. As you heal and mature, you may become attracted to people who are kind, sensitive, and helpful.

Remember that creating a solid support network requires time and effort. Be patient with yourself and do not be scared to ask for help.

Practicing mindfulness and meditation

Mindfulness and meditation are effective techniques for reconnecting with your inner strength. Mindfulness can help you focus on the present rather than worry about the future. Meditation can help you relax, reduce stress, and boost your general well-being.

Understanding the advantages of mindfulness is crucial. Mindfulness can help you reduce stress, improve focus, and increase emotional intelligence. It can also help you become more self-aware and compassionate.

Basic meditation techniques are relatively simple to master. Begin by locating a quiet spot to sit or lie down. Close your eyes and concentrate on your breathing. Pay attention to sensation 1 when you inhale and exhale. If your mind wanders, softly return your attention to your breathing.

Mindfulness in everyday life can be practiced in a variety of ways. You can practice mindfulness while eating, walking, or even doing the dishes. Pay attention to your body's sensations as well as the sounds around you. This can help you stay focused and less stressed.

One of the several advantages of mindfulness and meditation is that they reduce tension and anxiety. Regular mindfulness practice can help you learn to manage stress healthily. This can help you feel more relaxed, focused, and resilient.

Mindfulness and meditation also help increase self-awareness. Paying attention to your thoughts and feelings allows you to get a better understanding of yourself. This can help you make more informed decisions and have a more fulfilling life.

Embracing a growth mindset

A growth mindset is the concept that skills and intelligence can be developed with dedication and hard work. Adopting a growth mentality allows you to overcome two challenges, learn from mistakes, and reach your greatest potential.

Challenging fixed mindsets is the first step toward adopting a development mindset. A fixed mindset is the assumption that abilities are predetermined and cannot be altered. Recognizing and addressing these limiting ideas allows you to explore new possibilities.

Learning from failure is a vital component of human development. Instead of perceiving failures as setbacks, consider them chances to learn and improve. Analyze what went wrong and apply what you learned to improve your future performance.

Embracing challenges is another important part of a growth mentality. Instead of avoiding obstacles, view them as chances for learning and growth. Stepping outside of your comfort zone allows you to broaden your skills and attain greater success.

Developing a positive attitude is critical for sustaining a growth mindset. Focus on the positive things in your life and express thanks. A positive attitude can help you remain motivated and resilient in the face of adversity.

Believing in your abilities is critical for reaching your objectives. Believe in your abilities to learn and grow. With considerable effort and devotion, you can achieve everything you set your mind to.

25

Chapter 5

Visualizing Your Ideal Future

The path to a fulfilling life starts with a clear picture of where you want to go. Visualizing your perfect future is a powerful strategy for manifesting your aspirations. By taking the time to visualize your intended outcome, you may match your thoughts, emotions, and actions to create a reality that reflects your goals.

Setting ambitious objectives is a wonderful way to visualize your perfect future. Do not limit yourself to tiny, incremental measures. Instead, imagine large and set goals that will inspire and encourage you. When you aim high, you challenge yourself to achieve new heights.

A vision board is another effective way to envision your perfect future. You can construct a visual depiction of your dreams by collecting photos, phrases, and affirmations that correspond to your goals. This visual reminder might help you stay focused and inspired during your trip.

Affirmations are positive affirmations that can be used to alter your subconscious mind. Repeating affirmations daily might help you change your thinking and build a more positive approach. Choose affirmations that are meaningful to you and relevant to your goals. For example, if you want to boost your self-esteem, you could say something like, "I am confident and capable," or "I believe in myself."

Remember that visualization's power comes from inspiring imagination and action. By taking the time to imagine your perfect future, you may lay the groundwork for your success.

Action Steps

Once you have established a clear image of your ideal future, it is time to act. Breaking down your goals into smaller, more doable steps is an important method for reaching achievement. Focusing on one task at a time allows you to avoid feeling overwhelmed while maintaining momentum.

Prioritizing tasks is another necessary ability for effective action. Not all tasks are created equally. Some tasks are more significant than others, and some are more pressing than others. Prioritizing your duties will guarantee that you focus on the most important things first.

Time management skills might also help you stay on track. There are numerous time management approaches, including the Pomodoro Technique, the Eisenhower Matrix, and the Time Blocking Technique. Experiment with several ways to determine what works best for you.

Procrastination is a common roadblock that can slow progress. To overcome procrastination, it is necessary to discover the root causes. Are you terrified of failing? Do you feel overwhelmed? Are you simply uninterested in the task at hand? Once you have identified the root cause of your procrastination, you can devise tactics to overcome it.

Setting specific, measurable, attainable, relevant, and time-bound (SMART) goals will help you overcome procrastination. SMART goals provide a clear focus and keep you motivated.

Another effective technique is to implement a reward system. For example, you could give yourself a break or a treat after completing a specific activity.

Remember that action is the key to accomplishing your goals. Breaking down your goals into smaller steps, prioritizing your chores, efficiently managing your time, and overcoming procrastination will help you get closer to your perfect future.

overcoming obstacles.

The route to success is rarely straightforward. Challenges and setbacks are unavoidable. However, how you respond to these problems impacts your overall outcome. One of the most significant barriers to success is limiting beliefs. These are negative attitudes and beliefs that can prevent you from realizing your greatest potential.

To overcome limiting beliefs, it is necessary to question them. Ask yourself two questions: "Is this belief really true?" In addition, "What evidence do I have to support this belief?" By challenging your beliefs, you might start to recognize and replace negative thinking with positive ones.

Having a growth attitude is another important method for conquering problems. A growth mindset is the concept that you can improve your abilities and intelligence with work and practice. This perspective enables you to see problems as opportunities for growth and learning.

When faced with setbacks, it is critical to develop resilience. Resilience is the ability to recover from misfortune. Self-compassion is one strategy for increasing resilience. Be kind to yourself, even when things do not go as expected.

Seeking help from others is also necessary. Discuss your challenges with friends, family, or a therapist. Sharing your feelings can help you gain perspective and solve problems.

Remember that obstacles are a natural part of life. You can overcome any obstacle and achieve your goals by cultivating a growth mindset, confronting limiting beliefs, creating resilience, and seeking help.

Celebrating Your Achievements

Don't overlook your accomplishments, no matter how small. Recognizing your accomplishments, no matter how modest, can dramatically increase your motivation and self-esteem. When you celebrate your accomplishments, you reinforce favorable habits and establish a positive feedback loop.

Rewarding yourself is another excellent technique to recognize your accomplishments. This could range from taking a break to enjoying a favorite hobby or treat. Positive reinforcement can help you stay motivated and committed to your goals.

Sharing your accomplishments with others is an excellent way to rejoice. Sharing your accomplishments with friends, family, or colleagues can make you feel proud and validated. Furthermore, sharing your experiences might motivate others and strengthen relationships.

By taking the time to celebrate your accomplishments, you may keep a positive attitude and stay encouraged on your path to success. Remember that every step, no matter how tiny, helps you get closer to your final goal.

Creating a fulfilling life.

A fulfilling life is one filled with happiness, purpose, and meaning. Cultivating thankfulness is vital for creating such a lifestyle. By focusing on the positive aspects of your life, you may change your perspective and boost your overall happiness.

Self-care is an important aspect of living a fulfilling life. Taking care of your physical, mental, and emotional health is critical to your well-being. This could include things like meditation, yoga, exercise, or simply spending time in nature.

Strong relationships are also essential for leading a successful life. Nurturing your relationships with loved ones can offer you comfort, affection, and friendship. Strong relationships involve work, communication, and empathy.

Pursuing your passions is another way to have a fulfilling life. Doing what you enjoy can bring you happiness, fulfillment, and a feeling of purpose. Pursuing your hobbies, whether as a hobby, a career, or a volunteer activity, can greatly enrich your life.

Remember that a fulfilling life is a journey rather than a destination. You may live a truly meaningful and satisfying life by cultivating gratitude, practicing self-care, developing positive connections, and pursuing your hobbies.

26

Chapter 6

Setting Healthy Boundaries

Understanding the importance of boundaries.

Setting appropriate limits is frequently cited as a cornerstone of personal development and self-empowerment. It is like creating a strong fence around one's mental and psychological landscape, protecting oneself from unnecessary stress, manipulation, and the intrusion of toxic influences. Boundaries are more than just boundaries that separate us from others; they are guidelines that govern our interactions, ensuring that our wants, values, and well-being are met.

A lack of clear boundaries can result in a variety of issues. When we fail to set and maintain boundaries, we unintentionally invite others to overstep, abuse our weaknesses, and deplete our vitality. This might lead to feelings of bitterness, irritation, and emotional weariness. Furthermore, it can impede our ability to build true and lasting relationships since we may continuously compromise our own needs to suit the desires of others.

Consider the biblical tale of Jesus Christ to see how important limits are. Even though He was divine, He placed boundaries for His interactions with others. For example, when Jesus was tempted by Satan in the wilderness, He firmly refused the devil's temptations, responding, "It is written, 'Man shall not live by bread alone, but by every word that proceedeth out of the mouth of God.'" (Matthew 4:4). Jesus' capacity to withstand temptation and stay focused on His holy mission sprang from a deep grasp of His own identity and purpose.

Similarly, we must learn to identify our worth and set boundaries to ensure our well-being. This includes acknowledging our limitations, establishing priorities, and saying "no" when required. By doing so, we empower ourselves to live authentically and achieve our goals without jeopardizing our principles or our peace of mind.

Identifying your boundaries.

The process of determining your boundaries starts with self-awareness. To properly comprehend your limitations, you must go deeply into your psyche and examine your values, beliefs, and desires. What are your absolute must-haves? What are the lines you will not let others cross?

Consider the following questions to help you determine your boundaries:

1. What are my core values?
2. What are my wants and desires?
3. What are my limitations?
4. Which behaviors are unacceptable to me?
5. What are my triggers?

Once you have a positive awareness of yourself, you can start setting boundaries that are consistent with your beliefs and protect your well-being. Remember that your boundaries are personal and vary by situation and relationship.

Communicating Your Boundaries Effectively

Setting boundaries is just the first step. The next critical step is to communicate your boundaries clearly. This includes expressing your requirements and expectations in a clear and strong manner. Avoid passive-aggressive actions and unclear words. Instead, be upfront and specific about your expectations and what you will not tolerate.

For example, instead of saying, "I am feeling overwhelmed," you may add, "I am feeling overwhelmed right now, and I need some time to myself." This clear and aggressive communication helps others understand your needs and boundaries.

When communicating your boundaries, utilize "I" phrases to avoid seeming accusing or blaming. For example, instead of saying, "You always interrupt me," you may say, "I feel disrespected when I am interrupted." This technique focuses on your feelings rather than making broad generalizations or insulting the other.

Enforcing your boundaries

Setting boundaries is one thing; enforcing them is another. Once you have established your boundaries, stick to them, even if it is challenging. This could include saying "no" to requests, eliminating harmful relationships, or limiting how much time and energy you put into certain people.

Enforcing your limits demands guts and self-control. It may require difficulty or conflict, but the long-term advantages greatly outweigh the immediate difficulties. By regularly establishing your limits, you display self-respect and teach others how they should treat you.

Dealing with boundary violations.

Despite our best attempts, there may be moments when others cross our limits. When this happens, it is critical to remain cool and assertive. Avoid reacting impulsively or getting into conflicts. Instead, take a minute to evaluate the issue and decide the best course of action.

If the boundary breach is minimal, you may be able to resolve it directly with the person concerned. For example, if a buddy repeatedly cancels plans at the last minute, you could express your dissatisfaction and explain how it impacts you.

However, if the boundary breach is severe or recurring, you may need to take more significant measures, such as terminating the relationship or seeking help from a therapist or counselor.

Wise Decision Making

Recognizing Red Flags

Certain warning indicators in the complicated tapestry of human connections can indicate impending catastrophe. These red signs, which are typically inconspicuous at first, can develop into poisonous patterns of behavior if not addressed. Recognizing these signals allows us to protect ourselves from emotional injury and make educated decisions about who we invite into our lives.

One prominent red indicator is a desire to control behavior. A controlling partner may try to regulate your behavior, limit your social relationships, or monitor your activities. They may also use guilt trips, deception, or threats to maintain power and control. It is critical to remember that healthy relationships are based on mutual respect and trust, not dominance and force.

Another red flag is an absence of empathy. An empathic individual can comprehend and share the emotions of others. In contrast, a narcissist may be self-centered and unable to sympathize with the needs and emotions of others. They may ignore your emotions, ridicule your beliefs, or manipulate you into doubting your perceptions.

A history of abusive relationships is another major red flag. If someone has a history of mistreating their partners, they will likely repeat the same behaviors in subsequent relationships. This could include physical, emotional, or verbal abuse. It is critical to be aware of this red flag and avoid becoming associated with someone who has a history of abusive conduct.

Attracting Healthy Relationships

Attracting healthy partnerships necessitates a shift in perspective and a commitment to engage in personal development. By building self-love, self-respect, and self-awareness, we can attract others who share our values and are kind and compassionate.

Self-love is a key aspect in attracting healthy relationships. When we love ourselves, we have higher expectations for our relationships. We are less likely to tolerate harsh behavior or accept less than we deserve. To promote self-love, engage in self-compassion, positive self-talk, and gratitude.

Another important component is establishing appropriate limits. As previously said, boundaries are critical for ensuring our emotional and psychological well-being. Setting firm boundaries communicates our needs and expectations to others while discouraging them from taking advantage of us.

It is equally crucial to prioritize personal growth and development. Pursuing our passions, hobbies, and interests makes us more fascinating and attractive to others. We also gain confidence and self-esteem, which are necessary for developing strong, healthy relationships.

Screening Potential Partners.

When getting to know someone new, it is crucial to take your time and observe their behavior. Do not rush into a relationship because of physical attractiveness or superficial attributes. Instead, search for characteristics like kindness, empathy, honesty, and respect.

One method for screening possible partners is to monitor their interactions with others. Do they show their friends and family respect and kindness? Do they listen carefully and reply thoughtfully? Pay attention to how they deal with disputes and disagreements. Do they engage in blame, defensiveness, or aggression?

It is also critical to trust your instincts. If something feels wrong, it probably is. Do not dismiss your gut feelings, even if they appear unreasonable. Your intuition can be a useful tool for separating truth from falsehood.

Learning from Previous Mistakes

Everybody makes relationship mistakes, but we must learn from them and avoid repeating them. Reflecting on former relationships allows us to discover behavioral patterns and undesirable dynamics. We may learn from our experiences and make better decisions in the future.

One of the most common mistakes people make in relationships is ignoring warning signs. We may justify abusive behavior, make explanations for our partner's flaws, or hope that they will improve. People rarely change unless they are committed to doing so.

Another typical mistake is neglecting our own needs and desires to maintain the connection. This can lead to resentment, hostility, and, eventually, the end of the partnership. It is critical to prioritize our well-being and establish limits that safeguard our emotional and psychological health.

We may improve our chances of finding long-term love and happiness by learning from our failures and making deliberate decisions about who we let into our lives.

Communicating Effectively

Active Listening.

Effective communication is the foundation of any healthy relationship. It entails not only sharing our ideas and emotions but also actively listening to others. Active listening involves concentration, empathy, and patience. It entails listening carefully to what the other person is saying, understanding their point of view, and responding wisely.

To practice active listening, try the techniques below:

1. **Maintain eye contact:** This demonstrates your engagement and interest in the conversation.
2. **Avoid interrupting:** Let the other person complete speaking before reacting.
3. **Paraphrase and summarize:** Repeat what the other person stated in your terms to ensure comprehension.
4. **Ask clarifying questions:** If you are not sure about something, ask for clarification.
5. **Validate their feelings:** Recognize and validate the other person's emotions, even if you disagree with their viewpoint.

Active listening allows us to strengthen our relationships with others and settle disagreements more successfully.

Assertive Communication

Assertive communication is the ability to convey your demands and wants directly and courteously. It is a balance between passive and aggressive behavior. Passive communicators frequently avoid conflict and prioritize others' needs above their own. Aggressive communicators, on the other hand, prefer to dominate talks while ignoring the feelings of others.

Assertive communication includes:

1. **Using "I" statements:** "I feel" statements allow you to communicate your emotions without blaming others.
2. **Speaking simply and concisely:** Get to the point without rambling.
3. **Maintaining eye contact** indicates that you are confident and sincere.
4. **Using a calm and steady tone of speech:** Do not raise your voice or use angry language.
5. **Standing up for your rights:** Do not be hesitant to express your requirements and boundaries.

By using assertive communication, we may improve our relationships and reduce conflict.

Nonviolent Communication

Nonviolent communication (NVC) is an effective method for resolving conflicts and developing empathy. It includes four main components:

1. **Observations:** Describe the precise actions you see without passing judgment or appraisal.
2. **Feelings:** Recognize the emotions you feel as a result of the behavior.

3. **requirements:** Express any underlying requirements that are not being addressed.
4. **Requests:** Make specific requests to assist in meeting your needs.

Instead of saying, "You are always late," you could say, "When you are late, I feel frustrated and disrespected. I need to feel valued and respected; could you please try to be on time in the future?"

NVC allows us to convey our wants and feelings in a courteous and understanding manner.

Resolving conflicts constructively

Conflict is a normal element of any relationship. However, how we handle conflict has a big impact on the connection. Constructive conflict resolution includes:

1. **Maintaining calm:** Do not raise your voice or use frustrated language.
2. **Active listening** entails focusing on the other person's point of view.
3. **Using "I" statements:** Express your emotions without blaming or accusing.
4. **Keep the discourse focused on the problem**, not the other person's personality.
5. **Finding common ground:** Look for points of agreement and compromise.
6. **Seeking assistance if necessary:** If you are unable to resolve the problem on your own, consider consulting a therapist or mediator.

By addressing disagreement with a constructive perspective, we may deepen our relationships and create solutions that benefit everyone.

Communicating Your Needs and Wants

It is critical to communicate your requirements and desires clearly and assertively. Do not presume that others can read your thinking. Instead, explain your needs clearly and respectfully.

Here are some tips to express your demands and wants:

More details make it easier for others to understand your needs.

1. **Using "I" phrases** helps to avoid sounding accusatory or demanding.
2. **Be assertive, not aggressive:** Express your desires with confidence, but refrain from being confrontational or demanding.
3. **Be patient:** Others may need time to understand and respond to your demands.
4. **Do not be scared to negotiate:** Sometimes you will need to make concessions to obtain a mutually beneficial solution.

By properly expressing your needs and desires, you can improve your relationships and overall pleasure.

Developing Strong and Supportive Relationships

Cultivating empathy and compassion.

Empathy and compassion are necessary components for developing successful, supportive partnerships. Empathy is the ability to comprehend and share the emotions of another person. Compassion is the desire to relieve others' pain. By fostering these abilities, we can form stronger bonds with people and create a strong support network.

To increase empathy, try the following:

1. **Practice active listening:** Pay attention to what people are saying and strive to comprehend their point of view.
2. **Put yourself in their shoes:** Consider how you would feel if you were in their situation.
3. **Validate their feelings:** Recognize and validate their emotions, even if you disagree with them.
4. **Provide support and encouragement:** Show them that you care and are there for them.

Compassion, on the other hand, entails taking steps to alleviate others' pain. This could be lending a helpful hand, providing emotional support, or simply being present for someone in need. By exercising compassion, we can positively touch the lives of others while also strengthening our feelings of purpose.

Building trust and honesty.

Trust is the foundation of all excellent relationships. Building trust takes time and work, but it is ultimately worthwhile. Honesty and dependability are essential for building trust. Keep your promises, be open about your objectives, and refrain from lying or concealing information.

Honesty is vital for developing trust. Being honest shows respect and value for the relationship. It is critical to be honest about our feelings, thoughts, and objectives, even if it is challenging.

Being dependable is also essential for building trust. When we are reliable, we demonstrate that we can be relied on. This includes honoring our pledges, following through on our commitments, and being available to others when they need us.

Practicing forgiveness.

Forgiveness is the process of letting go of resentment and wrath. It is an extremely effective technique for healing and moving on from past hurts. When we forgive others, we are freed from the anguish and negativity of the past. This enables us to focus on the present moment and develop better, healthier connections.

Forgiveness does not imply forgetting what happened. It entails deciding to let go of the negative feelings linked with the experience. It is vital to remember that forgiveness is a decision, not an emotion. You may not want to forgive someone right immediately, but making a conscious decision to forgive allows you to begin to recover.

Offering support and encouragement.

Giving someone support and encouragement is an effective approach to demonstrate that you care. When someone is going through a difficult moment, lend a listening ear, a shoulder to weep on, or provide practical assistance. Make it clear to them that you are always available.

Encouragement is also an effective technique for encouraging and inspiring others. By encouraging others, we can help them attain their greatest potential. When someone is hurting, a simple word of encouragement can make a significant difference.

Nurturing Your Relationship

Nurturing solid, supportive relationships is essential for their longevity. This includes spending quality time together, conversing openly and honestly, and expressing gratitude to one another.

Spending quality time with your loved ones is one approach to strengthening your relationships. This includes putting your phones aside, turning off the television, and focusing on one another. You may go for a walk, eat together, or just talk.

Another strategy to strengthen your connections is to communicate openly and honestly. Share your thoughts, emotions, and experiences. Be a proficient listener and strive to grasp the other person's point of view.

Finally, express your gratitude for one another. Tell your loved ones how much you care about them. A simple thank you, meaningful praise, or a modest act of kindness can greatly deepen your relationships.

You can cultivate empathy and compassion, build trust and honesty, practice forgiveness, offer support and encouragement, and nurture your relationships to create a strong network of supporting friends and family. These relationships will give you love, support, and encouragement as you face life's obstacles.

Let Go of Toxic Relationships

Identifying Toxic Patterns

Toxic relationships can be emotionally taxing and damaging. It is critical to know the warning signals of a toxic relationship so that you can take action to break free. Some common indicators of a toxic relationship are:

1. **Constant criticism and judgment:** Your partner frequently criticizes your looks, behavior, or decisions.
2. **Gaslighting** is when your partner manipulates you into doubting your views and reality.

3. **Emotional abuse** occurs when your partner utilizes emotional manipulation, such as guilt trips or threats, to exert control over you.
4. **Control and possessiveness:** Your partner attempts to restrict your actions, limit your social relationships, or monitor your activities.
5. **Lack of respect:** Your partner disregards your boundaries, opinions, or emotions.
6. **Breaking Free of Toxic Ties**
7. **It's hard to leave a toxic relationship**, but you must take care of yourself. Here are several tips for breaking free:
8. **Set boundaries:** Communicate clearly with the toxic person and continuously enforce them.
9. **Limit interaction:** Avoid as much touch with the toxic individual as possible.
10. **Seek support:** Discuss your situation with friends, relatives, or a therapist.
11. **Focus on self-care:** Prioritize your physical and mental wellness through self-care activities.
12. **Avoid blaming yourself:** Remember that you are not accountable for others' poisonous actions.

Healing from the past

Healing from a toxic relationship requires time and effort. Here are some suggestions for healing.

1. **Self-compassion:** Be courteous and kind to yourself.
2. **Allow yourself** to be sad, angry, or confused.
3. **Seek professional assistance:** A therapist can help you work through your emotions and establish effective coping methods.
4. **Avoid concentrating on the past** and instead focus on the present. Instead, focus on the present moment.

5. **Create a support network:** Surround yourself with positive and encouraging individuals.

Moving Forward with Hope.

After leaving a toxic relationship, it is critical to focus on the future. Here are some tips to move forward with hope:

1. **Set goals:** Concentrate on your goals and aspirations.
2. **Practice thankfulness** by focusing on the positive things in your life.
3. **Use your past experiences to grow and learn.**
4. **Embrace new opportunities:** Be open to new experiences and connections.
5. **Believe in yourself:** Be confident in your abilities to overcome obstacles and create a satisfying life.

Accepting Solitude and Self-Sufficiency

Spending time alone can be an excellent opportunity for self-reflection and personal development. It is critical to embrace isolation and learn to like your own company. Here are some tips to embrace solitude:

1. Practice mindfulness by paying attention to your thoughts and feelings.
2. Engage in hobbies and interests: Do things that you enjoy.
3. Spend time in nature and connect with the natural world.
4. Read books to expand your knowledge and imagination.
5. Meditate to calm your mind and lessen tension.
6. By embracing isolation and self-sufficiency, you can lay a solid basis for future partnerships.

27

Chapter 7

Assessing Your Financial Situation

Taking stock of your financial situation is the first step toward financial empowerment. Start by making a complete list of your assets and liabilities. Assets are anything of worth that you own, including cash, savings accounts, investments, real estate, and personal things. In contrast, liabilities are your debts, such as credit card balances, student loans, mortgages, and vehicle loans.

Once you have a clear picture of your assets and obligations, it is important to assess your income and expenditures. Your income includes all forms of payment you receive, such as your salary, wages, rental income, and investment returns. Your expenses include the money you spend on numerous goods and services, such as accommodations, food, transportation, utilities, and entertainment. Budgeting tools, spreadsheets, and financial applications may all help you manage your income and expenses effectively.

Identifying and reducing excessive spending habits is an important step in reviewing your financial status. These habits can deplete your finances without adding much value. Impulsive purchases, excessive dining out, and multiple streaming service subscriptions are all common instances. By becoming more aware of your spending habits, you can pinpoint areas where you can cut back and save money.

Analyzing your debt is another critical stage in determining your financial health. Sort your loans into categories based on interest rates, repayment terms, and debt type. Prioritize high-interest bills, such as credit card debt, which can quickly accrue interest charges. Consider debt repayment tactics such as the debt snowball or debt avalanche approach for systematically paying off your bills.

Finally, take a minute to honestly evaluate your total financial situation. Do you feel content with your current financial situation? Are you saving enough for your future goals? Do you live within your means? Be open with yourself about your financial habits and activities. This self-assessment will help you find areas for growth.

Creating A Budget

A budget is a financial plan that allows you to manage your income and expenses, set financial objectives, and make sound decisions about how you spend your money. Creating a budget is an important step toward controlling your finances.

Begin by creating specific and attainable financial goals. Short-term objectives can include saving for a vacation or a new appliance, whereas long-term goals might include purchasing a home, retiring early, or paying for your children's school. Having precise goals will encourage you to stay within your budget and make compromises if necessary.

Budgeting tools and applications can help you precisely manage your income and expenses. These tools let you categorize your expenditures, set spending limitations, and track your progress toward your financial objectives. Mint, YNAB (You Need a Budget), and Quicken are among the most popular budgeting software.

Once you have a clear picture of your revenue and expenses, you can begin assigning money to other categories. Prioritize necessary expenses like shelter, food, and utilities. Set aside money for discretionary expenses like entertainment, dining out, and shopping. Be cautious of your purchasing patterns and avoid overpaying in any given category.

Remember, a budget is not set in stone. Life is full of surprises, including unanticipated expenses and income fluctuations. Be flexible and change your budget as necessary. Regularly examine and adjust your budget to ensure it is in line with your current financial status and goals.

By making and sticking to a budget, you may gain control of your finances, minimize financial stress, and work toward your financial goals.

Create an Emergency Fund

An emergency fund serves as a safety net for unexpected financial events such as job loss, medical problems, or car repairs. Creating an emergency fund is a critical step in securing your financial future.

Begin by selecting a realistic savings goal. Aim to save three to six months of living expenses. This money should cover basic expenses such as rent, utilities, groceries, and transportation.

Automate your savings to make them more manageable. Set up automated transfers from your checking account to your savings account on paydays. In this manner, you can save money without thinking about it.

If you want to save money quickly, consider cutting back on unneeded expenses. This could include lowering your dining out expenses, canceling unnecessary subscriptions, or finding cheaper alternatives to everyday things. You can also supplement your income with side hustles such as freelancing, tutoring, or selling products online.

Once you have established an emergency fund, you must safeguard it. Avoid using your emergency money for nonessential needs. Instead, place your emergency cash in a high-yield savings account or a short-term, low-risk investment.

Investing for Your Future

Investing is an effective way to increase your money over time. Investing your money allows you to earn returns that outpace inflation and help you achieve your financial goals.

Before you begin investing, it is critical to understand fundamental investment ideas. Stocks, bonds, and mutual funds are popular investing options. Stocks signify ownership in a firm, whereas bonds are loans to a company or the government. Mutual funds aggregate money from multiple participants to purchase a variety of securities, including stocks and bonds.

Diversifying your investments is critical for reducing risk. Diversification entails distributing your money among many asset classes and investment methods. Diversification reduces the impact of a single investment's negative performance.

If you are unsure about investing on your own, see a skilled financial counselor. A financial advisor can assist you in developing a personalized investment strategy that is aligned with your financial objectives and risk tolerance.

Remember, investing is a long-term plan. Avoid rash actions based on short-term market swings. Instead, concentrate on developing a well-diversified portfolio and adhering to your investment strategy.

By starting early and investing consistently, you can establish a sizable investment portfolio that will help you reach your financial goals.

Achieve Financial Independence

Many people aspire to be financially independent. It entails having the ability to live life on your own terms, without relying on a job or other external sources of income.

To obtain financial independence, you must first define it clearly for yourself. Are you looking to retire early? Would you like to travel the world? Or do you simply desire the freedom to follow your passions? Once you have identified your objectives, you may develop a specific financial strategy to assist you in achieving them.

Creating various revenue streams is an excellent technique for reaching financial independence. In addition to your regular employment, you may launch a side hustle, invest in rental properties, or generate passive income through web enterprises or royalties.

Debt reduction is critical for accelerating your route to financial independence. Pay off high-interest debt as soon as feasible and avoid incurring additional debt.

Finally, accumulating wealth over time is an important component of financial independence. Be patient and consistent in your savings and investments. Remember, riches are not created overnight. It requires patience, discipline, and a long-term view.

28

Chapter 8

Rediscovering Your Spirituality

Spirituality, which is frequently misinterpreted as merely religious affiliation, is an important component of the human experience. It includes our connection to something larger than ourselves, a sense of purpose, and a search for meaning. In terms of self-recovery, rediscovering our spirituality may be a powerful instrument for healing and transformation.

To begin this journey, we must first comprehend the nature of spirituality. It is not about sticking to rigid teachings or performing certain ceremonies. Instead, it is about developing a profound sense of inner serenity, compassion, and connection to the universe. It is about recognizing and developing our own and others' divine sparks via mindful activities and deliberate living.

Connecting with our inner selves is one of the most important techniques for recovering our spirituality. This entails interior reflection, paying attention to our ideas, emotions, and physical experiences. Through introspection, we can acquire vital insights into our deepest wants, fears, and goals. Journaling, meditation, and yoga are all effective strategies for supporting this process.

Journaling helps us to express ourselves freely and without criticism. It offers a secure environment in which to explore our inner world, uncover patterns, and obtain insight. Meditation, on the other hand, allows us to calm our minds and build a sense of inner serenity. It enables us to connect with our higher selves and reach deeper levels of consciousness. Yoga, a mind-body practice that includes physical postures, breathing exercises, and meditation, provides a comprehensive approach to self-care and spiritual development.

In addition to these practices, learning about various spiritual traditions and beliefs can help us gain a better understanding of spirituality. We can find inspiration in ancient wisdom, modern teachings, and varied cultural viewpoints. However, keep in mind that the ultimate goal is to build a personal relationship with the divine rather than adopting a certain belief system.

Practicing Mindfulness and Meditation

Mindfulness and meditation are key activities for achieving inner calm, lowering stress, and improving overall well-being. Being present at the moment allows us to fully enjoy life's joys and challenges without becoming preoccupied with anxiety or rumination.

Mindfulness, the discipline of paying attention to the present moment without judgment, can be applied to all aspects of our lives. It entails monitoring our ideas, emotions, and physical sensations with curiosity and acceptance. By practicing mindfulness, we can have a better understanding of our thoughts and behavior patterns, allowing us to make conscious decisions that are consistent with our beliefs.

Meditation, a practice that includes focusing the mind on a certain object, thought, or sensation, can help us relax and relieve tension. There are numerous types of meditation, such as mindfulness meditation, loving-kindness meditation, and mantra meditation. 1. Regular meditation practice can promote self-awareness, attention, and inner tranquility.

To incorporate mindfulness and meditation into our daily lives, we might begin with simple exercises such as attentive breathing and body scanning. Mindful breathing entails focusing on the experience of breath as it enters and exits the body. Body scans, on the other hand, require directing attention to various regions of the body one at a time. These techniques can be performed anywhere, at any time, and do not require any special equipment or instruction.

As we practice mindfulness and meditation more consistently, we may notice a shift in our perspective. We may develop more patience, compassion, and resilience. We may also feel a stronger sense of connectedness to ourselves and others. By adopting these behaviors, we can live more fulfilling and meaningful lives.

Cultivating gratitude.

Gratitude, or the practice of identifying and appreciating the positive things in our lives, is an effective approach to promoting pleasure and well-being. By focusing on the positive, we can change our viewpoint and feel more joy and happiness.

Keeping a gratitude journal is a simple way to practice gratitude. Every day, we can jot down a few things we are grateful for, no matter how insignificant they may appear. This exercise might help us build a more positive attitude toward life and appreciate the blessings we frequently take for granted.

Another excellent technique to cultivate thankfulness is to convey it to others. A simple "thank you" can go a long way toward building relationships and making people feel valued. We can also communicate gratitude by performing acts of kindness, such as volunteering, donating to a charity, or assisting a neighbor.

In addition to these techniques, we can promote appreciation by spending time in nature, practicing mindfulness, and doing things that make us happy. Connecting with the natural world allows us to have a better appreciation for the beauty and wonder of life. Mindfulness, or the discipline of being present at the moment, allows us to enjoy the basic joys of life and appreciate the beautiful things that are already there. Activities that provide us joy, such as hobbies, creative interests, or spending time with loved ones, can all improve our general well-being.

We can dramatically improve our lives by fostering thankfulness. Gratitude can help us overcome unpleasant emotions, reduce stress, and improve our overall physical and mental health. It can also improve our relationships, boost our resilience, and motivate us to lead more meaningful lives.

Seeking Meaning and Purpose.

The search for meaning and purpose is an essential human goal. It inspires us to explore the depths of our souls and connect with something bigger than ourselves. When we discover our purpose, we feel a sense of fulfillment and direction.

Identifying our values is one way we might uncover our mission. Values are fundamental ideas that shape our actions and judgments. Understanding our values allows us to match our lives with what is genuinely important to us. Consider people you like, events you enjoy, and causes you care about.

Once we know our values, we can set goals that reflect them. These goals can be large or little, immediate or long-term. The most important thing is that they are meaningful to us and add to our overall feeling of purpose. Setting and attaining goals helps us gain self-confidence and a sense of success.

Finding our life's purpose necessitates a greater level of introspection and self-discovery. It demands we think about our talents, skills, and passions. We may also need to experiment with alternative professional choices, volunteer opportunities, or hobbies to find our true calling. By connecting our hobbies to the needs of others, we might discover a feeling of purpose that goes beyond personal gain.

Remember that the path to discovering meaning and purpose is not always straightforward. There could be setbacks and hurdles along the way. However, by remaining focused on our values and goals, we may continue to progress. As we develop and mature, our sense of purpose may shift and deepen.

Connecting to a Higher Power

Connecting with a higher power is a very personal experience that can bring comfort, strength, and guidance. For many, it entails prayer, meditation, and a sense of spiritual belonging.

Prayer, a method of communicating with a higher power, can take various forms. Some people prefer structured prayers, while others prefer spontaneous expressions of thanksgiving, praise, or petition. Prayer can bring consolation, strength, and inspiration. It can help us feel connected to something bigger than ourselves and find calm amidst life's difficulties.

Meditation, a practice in which the mind is focused on a certain object, thought, or sensation, can also help us connect with a greater power. Meditation allows us to clear our minds, establish inner calm, and open ourselves up to spiritual experiences. Meditation is central to many spiritual systems.

In addition to prayer and meditation, engaging with nature can be an effective approach to communicating with a higher power. Spending time outside, whether hiking, gardening, or simply sitting in a park, can make us feel awed and amazed by the beauty and complexity of the natural world. It can also bring us closer to nature and its inhabitants.

Building ties with people who share our spiritual values can help us live more spiritually fulfilling lives. Joining a church community or spiritual group can lead to chances for worship, fellowship, and service. These connections provide us with support, encouragement, and a sense of belonging.

Finally, connecting with a higher power is a personal path that necessitates discovery and experimentation. There are no one-size-fits-all solutions. What works for one individual may not work for others. The most essential thing is to find practices that speak to you and help you feel more connected to something greater than yourself.

29

Chapter 9

Embracing the Power of Now

The present moment is a gift, a precious moment that passes through our fingers like grains of sand. However, we frequently find ourselves caught in the past, repeating old wounds and regrets, or eagerly anticipating the future, fretting about what might or might not happen. This persistent focus on the past and future deprives us of the joy and tranquility that can be experienced in the present moment.

Mindfulness, or the practice of being present at the moment, is an effective technique for reclaiming our lives and discovering true happiness. By focusing our attention on the present moment, we can break away from the loop of negative thoughts and feelings that so often hold us back. Mindfulness enables us to recognize the beauty and wonder of the present moment, regardless of how ordinary it appears.

When we are fully present, we may enjoy life with wonder and thankfulness. We can appreciate the little joys in life, such as the taste of a wonderful meal, the feel of the sun on our skin, or the sound of a loved one laughing. We can also connect more intimately with others since we are completely involved in the conversation and not distracted by our ideas.

One of the most significant benefits of mindfulness is its ability to help us let go of the past. Recognizing our prior experiences, both positive and negative, allows us to learn from them without becoming defined by them. We can let go of the emotional baggage we have been dragging around, making room for new experiences and chances.

When we are stuck in the past, we are unable to truly appreciate the present moment. We may find ourselves reflecting on past mistakes or hurts. This can trigger feelings of guilt, humiliation, and regret. By practicing mindfulness, we can learn to let go of negative feelings and go on with our lives.

Similarly, stressing about the future can keep us from completely experiencing the current moment. We can spend countless hours worrying about things that may or may not occur, such as job security, financial stability, or the health of our loved ones. Constant anxiety can hurt both mental and physical well-being.

By focusing on the present moment, we can lessen our worry and tension. We can be confident that we can handle whatever problems come our way. We can also learn to appreciate life's ambiguity, which is what makes it so thrilling and surprising.

To begin practicing mindfulness, we might focus on our breathing. We can stay present by focusing on our breath. We can also engage in mindfulness meditation, which is sitting quietly and concentrating on our breathing, thoughts, and feelings.

In addition to formal meditation, we can practice mindfulness in our daily lives by paying attention to our thoughts and emotions throughout the day. We can also practice mindfulness while performing regular tasks like eating, walking, or working.

Mindfulness can help us achieve more peace, joy, and fulfillment in our lives. We can learn to appreciate the beauty of the current moment while letting go of the past and future.

Let Go of the Past and Future.

As we have seen, mindfulness is an effective method for staying in the present moment. However, it is crucial to recognize that letting go of the past and future is not always simple. Our thoughts are naturally inclined to dwell on previous blunders or fret about future uncertainties.

To genuinely live in the present moment, we must learn to let go of these thoughts. One helpful strategy is to express thanks. By focusing on the positive aspects of our lives, we divert our attention away from negative ideas and emotions. Gratitude allows us to enjoy the current moment and acknowledge the blessings that we frequently take for granted.

Another beneficial technique is to accept the past. We can accept and learn from past mistakes instead of dwelling on them. Accepting our history allows us to release ourselves from the burdens of guilt and shame.

It is also vital to let go of any future expectations. Though goals and dreams are natural, we must not stick to them. Instead, we should accept the future's uncertainties and trust that everything will align.

We can practice mindfulness practices throughout the day to help us focus on the present moment. For example, we can pay attention to our senses when eating, relishing the flavor, smell, and texture of our food. We can also engage in mindful breathing, concentrating on the experience of our breath as it enters and exits our bodies.

Mindful walking is another great approach to being in the present moment.

We may calm our minds and enjoy peace and tranquillity by focusing on the sensation of our feet contacting the ground, the rhythm of our breath, and the sights and sounds around us.

As we practice mindfulness, we may notice that our thoughts wander less and less. When thoughts occur, we can gently focus our attention back on the present moment. We will gradually improve our ability to stay focused and present, allowing us to enjoy life more fully.

Remember that the journey of living in the present moment is an ongoing effort. There may be instances when our minds stray, and that is alright. The trick is to gently return our attention to the current moment, without judgment or self-criticism.

We can live a truly meaningful life by embracing the power of the present moment.

Embracing Imperfections

One of the most significant barriers to living in the present moment is the quest for perfection. We typically aim for perfection in our jobs, relationships, and appearance. However, the continuous quest for perfection can cause tension, anxiety, and disillusionment.

The truth is that perfection is an illusion. Nobody is flawless, and aiming for it is a useless undertaking. Accepting our flaws allows us to release ourselves from the burden of self-criticism and doubt.

Embracing imperfection is understanding our limitations and accepting ourselves as we are. It entails acknowledging that mistakes are a normal aspect of the human experience and that they can provide useful learning opportunities.

Instead of beating ourselves up for our mistakes, we can approach them with care and compassion. We can ask ourselves, "What can I learn from this experience?" and see it as an opportunity to progress.

Self-compassion is crucial for accepting imperfection. This entails treating oneself with the same compassion and understanding that we would show a friend. When we are fair to ourselves, we are more willing to forgive our mistakes and move forward.

Self-talk can help us create compassion for ourselves. Instead of criticizing ourselves, we might treat ourselves with care and encouragement. We can also practice self-care activities like taking a warm bath, reading a relaxing book, or spending time outside.

Accepting imperfection allows us to feel more free and at peace. We can let go of the need to have complete control and trust that everything will work out as planned. We can also embrace the beauty of our flaws and enjoy our uniqueness.

Remember that it is okay to make mistakes. It is acceptable to be imperfect. That is what defines us as humans. By accepting our flaws, we can live a more real and satisfying life.

Discovering Joy in the Little Things

In today's fast-paced world, it is easy to become caught up in the rush and bustle of daily life. We may find ourselves hurrying from one duty to the next, constantly pushing for more. However, the relentless pursuit of productivity can cause us to feel anxious, overwhelmed, and detached from ourselves and others.

To counterbalance this, we can develop a habit of finding delight in the smallest of things. We can create a stronger sense of happiness and well-being by focusing on the small moments of pleasure and thankfulness that occur throughout the day.

Gratitude is a simple approach to discovering joy in the little things in life. Taking time each day to be grateful shifts our focus from what we lack to what we have. This can help us recognize the gifts in our lives, no matter how tiny they may appear.

Another way to find joy in simple things is to relish pleasant experiences. When we relish a positive experience, we fully immerse ourselves in the present moment, focusing on the sights, sounds, and emotions that accompany it. This allows us to form enduring memories and increase our enjoyment of the experience.

For example, when we consume a meal, we can enjoy the flavors, textures, and scents of the food. We can also concentrate on our conversation and company. By completely participating in the activity, we can increase our enjoyment and create a positive memory.

In addition to relishing wonderful experiences, we can cultivate moments of joy in our daily lives. This could include walking through nature, listening to our favorite music, or spending time with loved ones. Making time for these things can help us improve our mood and reduce stress.

It is vital to remember that finding delight in the small things is a continuous process. It takes patience, perseverance, and a willingness to be present in the moment. By implementing these activities into our daily lives, we can achieve a higher level of happiness and well-being.

Creating a Meaningful Life

To live a truly fulfilling life, we must consider both our internal and external environments. While it is necessary to build inner peace and contentment, it is also critical to take concrete measures to create a life we enjoy.

One of the most crucial steps is to establish realistic goals. When we make specific and attainable goals, we give ourselves a sense of direction and purpose. We feel a sense of success and happiness when we achieve our aims.

It is also critical to prioritize self-care. We are better equipped to face life's obstacles and enjoy its pleasures if we take care of our physical, mental, and emotional needs first. This could include things like regular exercise, healthy nutrition, enough sleep, and spending time in nature.

Another important aspect of living a successful life is developing excellent relationships with people. Strong relationships offer us love, support, and companionship. By cultivating our ties with family, friends, and loved ones, we can build a strong social network that improves our lives.

Pursuing our passions and hobbies is equally important for living a fulfilled life. When we engage in activities we enjoy, we feel a sense of fulfillment and purpose. Pursuing our passions, whether it be painting, writing, gardening, or playing a musical instrument, can be quite rewarding.

Remember that leading a fulfilling life is a journey, not a destination. It is critical to be patient with ourselves and to acknowledge our accomplishments, no matter how minor. We may live a truly meaningful and fulfilling life by focusing on the present now, accepting imperfection, and finding delight in the little things.

30

Conclusion

Reclaiming Your Power

The path to restoring your power following narcissistic abuse is complex and frequently difficult. It takes strength, resilience, and a strong commitment to self-healing. Understanding the nature of narcissistic relationships, recognizing your worth, and implementing practical techniques will help you break free from the cycle of abuse and live a fulfilled life.

The first step toward reclaiming your power is to recognize the effects of narcissistic abuse on your emotional, psychological, and spiritual well-being. Narcissists frequently utilize manipulative strategies to dominate and abuse their victims, leaving them feeling confused, alone, and useless. It is critical to know that you are not alone and that many others have been through similar experiences.

One of the most prevalent narcissistic strategies is gaslighting, which is a type of psychological manipulation that causes you to question your reality. Narcissists can undermine your self-esteem and make you question your sanity by repeatedly dismissing your experiences, diminishing your feelings, and twisting the truth. Despite the narcissist's story, trust your instincts and believe in your version.

Another typical method is the silent treatment, which is a type of emotional abuse that can be as harmful as verbal or physical violence. Narcissists might punish you by withdrawing love and attention in response to perceived slights or conflicts. This can make you feel uneasy, uncomfortable, and desperate to get their acceptance. It is critical to realize that the silent treatment is a form of control, and you do not deserve to be treated like this.

Once you have acknowledged the effects of narcissistic abuse, you can begin the recovery process. This entails confronting the emotional suffering and trauma you have endured. Instead of suppressing your feelings, let yourself experience them. By acknowledging your grief, you may start to process it and move on.

One of the most effective strategies to recover from narcissistic abuse is to get professional therapy. A therapist can offer a safe and supportive environment in which to examine your emotions and build appropriate coping techniques. They can also assist you in identifying and addressing negative thought patterns that may be impeding your recovery.

In addition to treatment, numerous other self-help strategies can be useful. Journaling, meditation, yoga, and nature walks are a few examples. These exercises can relieve stress, boost mood, and increase general health.

As you start to heal, it is critical to work on regaining your self-esteem. Narcissistic abuse can undermine your self-esteem, making you feel undeserving of love and pleasure. By confronting negative self-talk and practicing self-compassion, you can start to develop a more positive self-image.

Setting and achieving personal goals might help enhance your self-esteem. This can boost your confidence and capabilities. Begin with small, attainable goals and progressively work your way up to larger ones. Celebrating your achievements, no matter how modest, can boost your sense of accomplishment.

Another key component of recovery is learning to establish and maintain appropriate boundaries. Narcissists frequently push boundaries, demanding your time, energy, and emotional support. Setting clear boundaries will protect you from potential harm and foster healthy relationships. This could include declining requests that do not line up with your values or priorities or restricting your interactions with toxic people.

As you recuperate, you may desire to reconnect with the narcissist. It is critical to fight this impulse. Continuing to interact with a narcissist might slow the healing process and set you back. It is critical to avoid interaction and focus on your well-being.

While the path to recovery may be difficult, know that you are not alone. By seeking help, practicing self-care, and using beneficial coping techniques, you can overcome the effects of narcissistic abuse and live a full life.

Maintaining Your Progress.

Once you have made substantial progress on your recovery journey, it is critical to keep going. This includes establishing techniques to prevent relapse and ensure long-term rehabilitation.

One of the most effective ways to make progress is to continue practicing self-care. This entails prioritizing your physical, emotional, and mental health. Engaging in enjoyable activities, such as hobbies, nature walks, or mindfulness practice, can help alleviate stress and increase general well-being.

It is also necessary to set healthy limits with people. This entails setting boundaries for what you will and will not tolerate from others. Establishing clear boundaries allows you to protect your energy and prevent harmful connections. You can decline requests that don't fit your priorities or values.

Another important aspect of maintaining development is building a solid support system. Surrounding oneself with positive and supportive individuals can help you get encouragement, empathy, and understanding. Consider joining a support group or obtaining therapy to connect with others who have been through similar circumstances.

It is critical to be aware of the warning signals of relapse. These could include increased anxiety, despair, or feelings of isolation. If you observe any of these symptoms, you must take steps to address them. This could include obtaining professional help, contacting a trusted friend or family member, or engaging in self-care activities.

One of the most typical mistakes in recovery is idealizing the narcissist. This happens when you start romanticizing the relationship and forget about its negative features. It is critical to remind yourself of the reasons you left the relationship and concentrate on the positive aspects of your life.

To avoid idealization, keep a journal or log of the narcissist's harmful actions. This can act as a reminder of the reality of the connection, allowing you to avoid sliding back into previous behaviors.

It is vital to acknowledge and appreciate your progress while you heal. Recognize your achievements, no matter how minor. This might increase your self-esteem and encourage you to keep pushing forward.

Remember that the path to healing is not always linear. There could be difficulties along the road. However, by remaining devoted to your healing goals and seeking help, you may overcome any challenges and emerge stronger than before.

Inspiring Others

Sharing your narcissistic abuse stories and recovery path can be a tremendous source of inspiration for others. You can help others break free from toxic relationships by providing hope, support, and direction.

Speaking publicly about your experience is a powerful influencer. This can be accomplished via writing, speaking, or creating internet material. Sharing your stories can assist in normalizing the topic of narcissistic abuse and reducing its stigma.

When telling your narrative, it is critical to be honest and real. Do not be scared to express your vulnerabilities and emotions. Being open and honest allows you to connect with others on a deeper level and provide true assistance.

It is equally crucial to consider the impact of your words. Do not blame or shame the narcissist. Instead, focus on your own experiences and lessons learned. By telling your story with love and compassion, you can help others heal and grow.

In addition to sharing your story, you can encourage others by providing practical advice and support. This could include giving materials such as books, articles, or online communities. You can also provide emotional support by listening to others' tales and delivering encouraging comments.

One way to provide practical guidance is to share information on how to recognize and avoid narcissistic relationships. This could include explaining red flags like love bombing, gaslighting, and triangulation. By educating people on the symptoms of narcissistic abuse, you can help them protect themselves from future harm.

Another way to assist is to establish a secure and supportive community. This can be accomplished using internet forums, support groups, or social media groups. Connecting with those who have had similar experiences allows you to provide mutual support and encouragement.

Remember that your journey to recovery serves as a strong example for others. By sharing your story and offering assistance, you may help countless people break free from poisonous relationships and enjoy fulfilled lives.

A brighter future awaits.

As you continue your healing and growth path, remember to look ahead to the possibilities that await you. You may make your future brighter by adopting a positive mindset and making goals.

Visualization is one of the most effective techniques for shaping a positive future. Imagining your ideal life can motivate you to achieve it. Visualize yourself in a loving and supportive relationship, living in a lovely home, and pursuing your dreams.

Setting objectives is another important step toward a brighter future. Breaking down your long-term goals into smaller, more manageable tasks allows you to stay motivated and track your progress. Celebrate your victories, no matter how minor, and use them as motivation to keep going.

It is vital to realize that the path to healing is not always straightforward. There could be setbacks and hurdles along the way. However, by remaining focused on your goals and practicing self-compassion, you can overcome any challenges.

As you heal and evolve, you may become drawn to new opportunities and experiences. Be open to these chances and seize them with excitement. Remember: life is a journey, not a destination. Embrace every moment and treasure the opportunities that come your way.

By concentrating on the good, making objectives, and seizing new possibilities, you may shape a future full of love, joy, and fulfillment. Remember that you deserve happiness, and you have the ability to create it.

A final word of encouragement.

Remember that you are not alone on this changing path. Millions of people worldwide have suffered the agony and destruction of narcissistic abuse. Your strength, healing, and growth are underestimated.

Accept the obstacles as opportunities for progress. Every challenge you face will help you grow stronger and more resilient. Do not be afraid to ask for support from friends, family, or professionals. A robust support system can significantly improve your healing process.

Remember that how the narcissist perceives you does not define your worth. You are precious, worthy of love and happiness. As you heal, you will rediscover your true self and find the joy and fulfillment you deserve.

Believe in yourself and never give up hope. Your future is bright, and the best is still to come.